SEXUAL ANALYSIS OF
DICKENS' PROPS

SEXUAL ANALYSIS OF

DICKENS' PROPS

**ARTHUR
WASHBURN
BROWN**

EMERSON BOOKS, INC.
New York

MANUFACTURED IN THE UNITED STATES OF AMERICA

CONTENTS

PREFACE

IT WAS SOME years ago in a doctoral seminar presided over by Susanne Nobbe that I first read all of Dickens' novels all the way through. Mrs. Nobbe suggested for the seminar paper that I might see what, if anything, Dickens did with the symbol of fire. I decided then that he had done little that was unexpected with it, but it was at that time that I developed the painstaking technique of going through the novels page by page and noting down on 3" by 5" slips of paper every reference to fire. When I came much later to work on the props in Dickens' novels I employed the same technique, and consequently amassed upward of 25,000 such slips of paper. It is out of the foundation provided by this mass of material that the observations in the following pages are drawn.

One consequence of this is that the more intimate and detailed a knowledge of Dickens' novels the reader has, the more illuminating will he find the pages of the following book. Nevertheless it seems to me that in addition to being of use to the most deeply committed Dickens enthusiast and scholar, the following chapters may prove interesting and valuable also to the person whose acquaintance with Dickens is at this point more modest.

In addition to serving the expert interests of the confirmed Dickens *aficionado,* this book ought to be of value to the person who has read only a few of Dickens' novels, and who has perhaps even forgotten some of these. He doubtless plans to read more of Dickens when time permits. Such a person may have read *A Tale of Two Cities* and *David Copperfield,* and possibly *Great Expectations.* Perhaps *Hard Times* and *Oliver Twist* might also be added to this list of familiar works for the seriously interested amateur. For those who want to pursue Dickens beyond these basic five, I should recommend gradually adding *Bleak House* and *Martin Chuzzlewit* and *Little Dorrit,* and then either *Nicholas Nickleby* or *Barnaby Rudge,* and, of course, ultimately all the rest.

In the appendix to this book I have summarized six of the novels for the convenience of those whose memory of them is vague or who have never had the chance to read them. Two of these novels, the *Old Curiosity Shop* and *Our Mutual Friend,* are little read nowadays, but some familiarity with them is very important to what I have to say here. I should strongly suggest that the reader who is unacquainted with them read these two summaries before proceeding further.

This book does not attempt to be well balanced or well rounded in its approach to Dickens. The psychoanalytic view provides a very powerful lens through which one can see a great deal of detail in a very narrow range. An analysis of the props in the novels constitutes an especially narrow and specialized focus for that lens. It *does* provide an especially useful way of revealing meaning in Charles Dickens' fiction which one might not ordinarily know was there. It is a view of Dickens which does not emphasize the great social critic, rhetorician, dramatist, humanitarian, comic artist, and even novelist that he was.

The meaning of the individual props derives, of course, from the context in which they occur. If one collects all of the instances of the occurrence of an individual kind of prop from all the novels in which they appear, lifts them out of context, and regards them as a group, then one can begin to see dimensions of meaning in the props which are sometimes surprisingly revealing. If one applies this

newly discovered meaning to each instance of the occurrence of a prop in a specific novel one can then discover
a great deal that is new and unsuspected about what is
going on in each novel in particular and in Dickens' fiction
in general.

The method of approach in the following pages is thus
a circular one which is, so to speak, always in motion. It
is forever moving from specific, detailed references to objects and occurrences in a particular novel, to generaliza-
tions which can be made about that kind of object or event
in all of the novels, and then back again to the application
of the generalization to the particular novel with which the
cycle started. Our view will oscillate from one or another
of Dickens' novels to a brief but very narrow view of all
of his novels taken together and then back again to one
or another specific novel. The ultimate end to be achieved,
however, will be a new and greatly enlarged understanding of each of Dickens' novels taken by itself in isolation
and also of all of Dickens' novels taken as a complete
canon.

In addition to Susanne Nobbe my most extensive intel-
lectual indebtedness for the following book is to Alice
Green Fredman and Steven Marcus. Mr. Marcus in particular suggested the application of psychoanalytic methods
to Dickens, and supplied in his own work models of how
it might best be done.

To my friend Christopher Mulvey I owe a debt more
difficult to define. We speak the same language where
Dickens is concerned, and in our numerous conversations
about him it has often proven impossible to distinguish
just where his ideas leave off, and mine begin.

I owe a further debt to my wife, Diana. Without her
sacrifice and support the following book could not have

been written. She maintained the family, and often my morale as well, through all of the years I have given mostly to Dickens' props.

There is still another kind of debt I owe to my authors. Both Sigmund Freud and Charles Dickens are fun to read. As important as Freud is as the seminal thinker who created a new approach to the study of the mind, the fact is often obscured that he is a first rate writer and a first rate literary critic in his own right. And of Dickens all I can say is that the better I have come to know him, the more I have come to love, admire, and respect him. As I read the novels over and over and over again, I learned more emphatically that the Dickens novel I love the best is the one I happen to be reading at the moment. One sure symptom of true preeminence of literary genius is that the work never palls. Familiarity does not breed contempt; rather it raises up new riches. Through the days, weeks, and months of discouragement (when this topic seemed to be nothing more than a form of dull idiocy), Charles Dickens was always revealing new subtleties of artistry and meaning, always able to make me laugh *again,* always making my book about him rewarding to me in spite of myself.

SEXUAL ANALYSIS OF
DICKENS' PROPS

CHAPTER I

A HUNDRED THOUSAND
GAMES

Why Cribbage
Represents Sexual Intercourse

THE NOVELS OF Charles Dickens are crowded not only with people but also with specific, concrete objects. If the novels' pages were a stage, these objects would be regarded as props. These things often seem to serve the same sort of function in Dickens' fiction that they would serve in a dream. They sometimes appear to be focal or gathering points for a good deal more meaning than their first, relatively innocent impression provides. These apparently innocuous props supply considerable information about what is going on in the novels under the surface.

The application of psychoanalytic methods in the critical examination of fiction no longer constitutes the novelty it once did. This is especially true for Charles Dickens. His work readily lends itself to the application of methods of analysis like those Sigmund Freud applied to dreams. Critical studies of Dickens by Edmund Wilson and Steven Marcus have demonstrated this to be a fruitful approach.

The method employed to expose the hidden meaning is analogous to that which Freud adopted in the interpretation of dreams. Here the analysis will focus upon the interpretation of a large number of specific references in the novels to certain kinds of props.

The best procedure, of course, would be to psychoanalyze Dickens at the same time we analyze the props, as Steven Marcus does in "Who is Fagin?" But practical problems as well as analytical considerations prevent this. We very often do not have the necessary biographical information. Although it would undeniably be helpful to have, it is not essential to the analysis of the fiction itself.

It is possible to illustrate this point with some of the same material Mr. Marcus employs in the explication of Fagin. The fact that a profound trauma was created in Dickens as a child by his brief employment at Warren's Blacking undoubtedly contributes to an understanding of references to shoe blacking, shoes, and related matters in the novels. Although in many ways an amiable man, Dickens' father had never been a particularly good provider. Shortly before Charles' twelfth birthday the family fortunes were in such a state of decline that a number of retrenchments were called for. The Dickens family moved into cheaper and meaner lodgings.

Although a scholarship enabled Charles' musically talented older sister to attend school, there was no money for Charles' education and he remained at home in idleness except for menial tasks like polishing his father's shoes. Soon a well meaning relative provided a job for the boy attaching labels to jars of shoe blacking. He worked in the cleanest part of the factory, the job paid reasonably well for the level of skill involved, and it was a not inappropriate mode of employment for a poor boy without expectations of rising in life. But the sensitive young prodigy, always ambitious, was convinced that with the proper education he would achieve great things in life. At Warren's Blacking he felt utterly abandoned and cast away by his parents and by life. Shortly thereafter his father was imprisoned for debt and matters looked dark indeed.

So deeply did Dickens feel the shame and degradation of this period of his life that he kept the memory completely secret even from his own family. Only after Dickens' death did John Forster, the one closest friend to whom Dickens had confided the secret, reveal the story to the world in his biography of the great author.

But even if John Forster had not revealed the immense significance of this even in Dickens' life, it would still be possible inductively to see that all references to shoe blacking in the novels are charged with emotions of degradation and shame. The most explicit and the most nearly autobiographical reference appears in *David Copperfield*. David's hated stepfather has exiled him to Murdstone and Grinby's once David's mother's death has relieved Mr. Murdstone of any sense of obligation to further David's education. Here David is employed with certain other men and boys to examine a great many empty wine bottles against the light

and to reject those that were flawed, and to rinse and wash them. When the empty bottles ran short, there were labels to be pasted on full ones, or corks to be fitted to them, or seals to be put upon the corks, or finished bottles to be packed in casks.

"No words can express the secret agony of my soul as I sunk into this companionship. . . ." said a perfectly miserable and desolate David, speaking for Charles Dickens as well as for himself, as John Forster makes quite clear in his biography. In his heart Dickens blamed his parents for being thus sunk. His feelings toward them are expressed in David's situation in the novel. The father has been replaced by a monstrous stepfather. The once-loving mother has been killed off. Dickens seems to have associated the sense of abandonment and degradation in this experience with his father's contrasting warm appreciation of his son's youthful ability to sing comic songs. The emotions of shame appear, therefore, in association with occasional references to verbal wit. Freud makes quite clear that there need not necessarily be anything logical about the connections between one perception and another in memory. The mere fact that the perceptions occurred at the same time is enough to associate them with each other.

In *Pickwick Papers,* the first of Dickens' novels, Mr. Pickwick elevates Sam Weller out of a degraded social position into the second most important character of the novel. Scarcely any social rank is more humble than that of a bootblack. Sam had occupied the position of "boots" at the White Hart Inn where Mr. Pickwick first encountered him, and where the polish he produced with Day and Martin would strike "envy to the soul of the amiable Mr. Warren." Later in the same book Tony Weller cautions his son against excessive verbal wit when Sam is composing a valentine:

> poetry's unnat'ral; no man ever talked
> poetry 'cept a beadle on boxin' day,
> or Warren's blackin', or Rowland's oil,
> or some o' them low fellows.

Mr. Pott, the editor of the Eatanswill Gazette suffers from the rivalry of the editor of the Eatanswill Independent, Mr. Slurk. That gentleman, among other unpleasant qualities, has "very stiff black hair cut in the porcupine or blacking-brush style."

Many of the references are simply associated with circumstances of social degradation, disgrace, or poverty. In the second novel, *Oliver Twist,* the "porochial" surgeon's apprentice sends an impoverished woman (whose debased social standing cannot be accorded better medical care) some medicine in a blacking-bottle. Beadle Bumble is outraged because the woman says it is not the proper medicine for her complaint and refuses to take it. In the same novel flash Toby Crackit, who is not only at the bottom of the social scale by virtue of his being a criminal, but is, moreover, a poverty-stricken criminal hard-up for work, complains to Fagin that his top-boots have had "not a drop of Day and Martin . . . not a bubble of blacking."

In *Nicholas Nickleby* you know that in Newman Noggs' house the poverty of the inmates increases as you go upstairs. The furniture on each successively higher landing gradually deteriorates until the garret landing-place, where Newman lives, "displays no costlier articles than two crippled pitchers, and some broken blacking-bottles." Again in *Nicholas Nickleby* while praising the rusticity of the city, Tim Linkinwater almost draws back from telling Nicholas about the flowers he can see growing in the back-attic win-

dow, at No. 6, in the court, because of the shameful
absurdity of their immediate environment:

> "There were hyacinths there this last spring, blossom-
> ing in—but you'll laugh at that."
> "At what?"
> "At their blossoming in old blacking-bottles," said Tim.
> "Not I, indeed," returned Nicholas.

In the *Old Curiosity Shop* there is Mr. Slum's acrostic on
the name "Warren" that he wants to convert and sell to
Mrs. Jarley for advertising purposes. His very name conveys the lowness of the verbal cunning with which he
strives to eke out his precarious living. In *Barnaby Rudge*
one of the three primary scenes of spectacular destruction is "the Warren." It is a location which provides a
focal point both for the prejudice against Catholics which
underlies the Gordon Riots, and for the guilt which haunts
Barnaby's ghost-like father. There is also in the same novel
the insult of becoming a shoe-black added to the injury of
Simon Tappertit's losing both legs.

In *David Copperfield,* when David visits his struggling
young friend Traddles in the latter's lodgings at chronic
debtor Micawber's house (a clear case of the poor housing
the poor), he observes that Traddles keeps "his blacking-
brushes and blacking . . . among the books—on the top
shelf, behind a dictionary." Traddles is studying law, and
this is an interestingly literal degradation of words.

In the window of the rag and bottle shop of Mr. Krook,
a location and character which symbolically represent the
wickedness and squalor of chancery law in *Bleak House,*
there were "quantities of dirty bottles: blacking bottles,
medicine bottles, ginger-beer and soda-water bottles,
pickle bottles, wine bottles, ink bottles." It is worth noting

that here both David Copperfield's shameful wine bottles and Charles Dickens' degrading blacking-bottles appear in the same location. An additional cause for young Charles' sense of shame was the fact that for a time he labelled the blacking bottles in a window, on public display.

In *Hard Times,* Mr. Bounderby, always out to exaggerate the humbleness of his origins, claims that for years the only pictures he ever had were the engravings which depicted a man shaving himself in a boot on the blacking bottles he used in cleaning boots, and that he sold afterwards for a farthing apiece. It is the picture on the label that is of central importance here. There is a further curiously inverted relationship between Mr. Bounderby and his author. Charles Dickens kept the lowlife blacking bottle episode strictly in the dark and made public only the more elevated aspects of his essentially middle class background. Mr. Bounderby, however, maintained pretensions of early gutter poverty much lower than anything Dickens had actually known. He kept completely in the dark the fact that his early childhood had actually been mostly lower middle class just like Dickens'.

When Dickens' father was imprisoned for debt while his son was laboring in sorrow at Warren's Blacking, he was placed in the primary London debtors' prison, the Marshalsea. *Little Dorrit* is Dickens' major novel about imprisonment for debt and its spiritually and psychologically destructive effects. In this book, among the nondescript messengers of the Marshalsea, the poor who served the even poorer debtors, the one Arthur Clennam speaks to "had two red herrings in his hand, and a loaf and a blacking brush under his arm."

The primary father figure in *Little Dorrit* is Mr. William Dorrit who is, indeed, known as "the father of the

Marshalsea." Bright young Ferdinand Barnacle explains William Dorrit's original financial failure, which has something of the force of original sin attached to it, as having been due to his being a partner "in a house in some large way—spirits, or buttons, or wine, or blacking" when "the house burst." Here again wine and blacking appear together as they often do in the novels which Dickens wrote after *David Copperfield*. It was this novel in which he indelibly associated his own feelings about blacking with David's feelings about wine.

In *Great Expectations,* when Joe Gargery and Mr. Wopsle arrive in London they look at the "Blacking Ware'us" and decide it does not come up to its likeness in the red bills in the shop doors "as it is there drawd too architectooralooral." This is a curious sort of shrine for a tourist to visit, of course, except for Joe's intimate association with what Pip regards as his own low social origin. We shall later have occasion to observe that Pip's *black*smithing, with its possible punning association with *blacking,* joins David Copperfield's employment at Murdstone and Grinby's in its displaced reference to the author's sense of shame for his days at Warren's Blacking.

In *Our Mutual Friend,* the last novel Dickens completed, Reginald Wilfer, the father of the heroine, is the victim of his wife and circumstances. He is so poor that he "performed with a blacking-brush on the family's boots, instead of performing on enormous wind instruments."

In *The Mystery of Edwin Drood,* the novel Dickens was writing when he died, Choirmaster John Jasper stops at a "hybrid hotel" which does not expect him "to order a pint of sweet blacking for his drinking, and throw it away." He may "have his boots blacked instead of his stomach." And here again we see the clear identification of wine and blacking. It is worth observing, further, that the

association of poverty and degradation with the polishing
of shoes was not an idiosyncrasy of Dickens alone. It was
the case then, as, indeed, now, that the poor and humble
did the job.

We do have biographical information regarding the
significance of shoe polishing to Dickens. We could, however, derive the emotional overtones of shame and degradation, coupled, occasionally, with ideas of verbal wit,
from the references themselves. But if we turn to a prop
for which there is no known biographical association, it is
still possible to collect all of the references in the texts of
the novels, and, through their analysis to arrive at unsuspected meaning in them. We shall do this despite the fact
that the individual occurrences of the prop may appear
entirely innocuous and insignificant. Indeed, Freud does
point out that it is precisely the most trivial elements of
a dream which are indispensable to its interpretation.

Cribbage is an innocent game which involves sticking
little wooden pegs into little wooden holes. Draughts, or
backgammon, also involves wooden pieces, or counters, but
they are flat and do not go into anything. After a certain
critical moment all of the cribbage games in Dickens'
novels are played in the presence of sexually paired couples
between whom there either is or is soon anticipated to be
frequent sexual intercourse. Sometimes the couples are
themselves the players. They are, in any case, always present. By contrast, backgammon is invariably played by
people between whom there is not and will not be any
sexual relationship.

There are three cribbage games which occur in the
novels before the sexual association is established, and they
are quite free of any such hidden meaning. In Dickens'
second novel Mr. Brownlow's old lady housekeeper teaches
Oliver Twist cribbage to help him while away the time

Dick Swiveller Introduces the Marchioness to Purl and Cribbage

during his convalescence. Toby Crackit and Mr. Chitling pass the time by playing the game in Fagin's lair in the same novel. Finally, there is a four-handed game involving Daniel Quilp, Richard Swiveller, Mrs. Quilp, and Fred Trent in the *Old Curiosity Shop*.

It is in this last novel that the critical occurrence which irrevocably establishes the sexual association with cribbage occurs. Indeed, it is Dick Swiveller who establishes it, and he does so with the Marchioness. It all begins when Dick decides to risk the vengeance of Sally Brass and to release the little female servant from her underground prison. On that occasion he feeds her beef and ambrosial beer, he confers upon her the name of "Marchioness," and he teaches her to play cribbage. Later when Sampson Brass has fired him, he suffers a protracted illness from which he will arise a wiser and better man. He slowly awakens from his feverish delirium to find the Marchioness "playing cribbage with herself at the table."

> There she sat, intent upon her game, coughing now and then in a subdued manner as if she feared to disturb him— shuffling the cards, cutting, dealing, playing, counting, pegging—going through all the mysteries of cribbage as though she had been in full practice from her cradle!

And, again, much later on it is a part of the happy ending of the concluding chapter that the Marchioness "was ever a most cheerful, affectionate, and provident wife" to Dick, while he "was to her an attached and domesticated husband."

> And they played many hundred thousand games of cribbage together.

As suggestive as that is by itself, its meaning is really revealed only by the confirmation of all of the succeeding games of cribbage in the novels. In *Martin Chuzzlewit,* for example, Charity Pecksniff rallies Augustus Moddle out of his state of depression over losing the love of her sister, Merry, by challenging him to cribbage. When Mrs. Todgers suggests they play "for love" he changes color. Charity and Augustus do become engaged. Their anticipated union is never consummated. But at the time of the cribbage the anticipation is still there.

In *Dombey and Son,* when Toots plays cribbage with Captain Cuttle, he has the aid of Susan Nipper whom he will shortly marry. And in *David Copperfield,* during the game of cribbage Traddles and Copperfield play, Dora is sitting nearby playing her guitar and singing so that "it seemed to me as if our courtship . . . were not yet over."

The evidence of backgammon provides an entirely consistent contrast. In *David Copperfield,* David's maiden Aunt Betsey plays backgammon with her ward, Mr. Dick. In the same book Steerforth and Rosa Dartle play backgammon. Although she clearly entertains a fierce sexual desire for him, and they may have had a previous affair, at the time of the backgammon Steerforth is ruthlessly and sadistically engaged in frustrating her completely. In *Bleak House* Esther Summerson plays backgammon with John Jarndyce, and although at one point he proposes marriage, it is quite clear that he would not expect her to fulfill any functions other than strictly housekeeping ones. In *Hard Times* Mrs. Sparsit, who would *like* to marry Mr. Bounderby, plays backgammon with him. "Miss Gradgrind" whom Bounderby *does* marry isn't interested in backgammon. In *A Tale of Two Cities* Mr. Lorry the banker plays backgammon with Dr. Manette, and in *Our Mutual Friend* Bella Wilfer plays the game with her sister Lavvy, and in

Edwin Drood Mr. Sapsea plays the game with Mr. Jasper.

Here again it is possible to see that there is underlying meaning in Dickens' use of cribbage just as there is in his use of boot blacking. The briefest kind of reference to the occurrences of props in the novels, taken almost entirely out of the context, can reveal the existence of a substratum of meaning. It is meaning which either does not appear at all when the individual instances of the props are encountered one by one in the context of their novels, or it is meaning which appears so faintly as easily to be missed. Unlike the collective significance of the blacking references the collective significance of the cribbage and backgammon games is quite evident without the benefit of any biographical reference to the author's own experience of these games.

Thus far, all that has occurred is a collection of the evidence which has been allowed to speak for itself. We have not really analyzed it at all. We have not made any attempt to discover what the novels can reveal about the reasons for such meaning to attach to cribbage in the way and at the time that it does.

The sexual connotations of cribbage clearly become established with Dick Swiveller and the Marchioness, and it is with them that any analysis of it must begin. Since the analysis is to be made after the manner of Freud's analysis of dreams, it is important to bear in mind certain of the principles he established and observed. Among these, for instance, is the principle that one dream person is sometimes reincarnated in another dream person by means of the functions or relationships involved. One figure can represent several persons by appearing in the roles or functions of all of them, or several figures can represent a single person. The ego of the dreamer, or author, can represent itself both directly and indirectly through identification with a single person or with a variety of different persons within the story. This latter feature of dream activity enables the dreamer to express a part of himself with which he does not wish to be directly associated through a separate dream character. Indeed, friends and enemies can be reincarnated in dream persons either independently of one another, or, if it suits the dream work better, in the same person.

Throughout his novels Dickens employed the technique of reduplicating particular characters or situations several times over with slight variations in the same book. This way the various diverse ramifications of a particular person or problem could be elaborated with more detail and psychological complexity than would be possible if the character or problem were rendered only once. We shall be seeing a lot of this sort of thing.

Dick Swiveller and the Marchioness represent more than just themselves. Although their relationship is one of the few charming and delightful things in an otherwise unhappy and even depressing novel, they are far from being the central figures of the *Old Curiosity Shop*. In the total psychic economy of the novel their initially apparent value is modest. This novel is essentially the story of Ellen Trent, who is better known as Little Nell. She is more nearly in late childhood than early adolescence, and has a rather extraordinarily unearthly, spiritual beauty. Little Nell, an incarnation of perfect goodness and purity, is relentlessly pursued and hounded by evil forces through a cruel and wicked world. She finally escapes in death after suffering one of the most protracted illnesses in all literature.

Dick Swiveller and the Marchioness are minor characters. Although they are instrumental in bringing about the downfall of the principal villains, the moneylender, Daniel Quilp, and the lawyers Sampson Brass and his sister Sally, their direct contact with Little Nell is very slight, indeed. But as happens in dreams there has been a transference and displacement of psychical intensities from elsewhere to give them a new value of such importance that their author's mind, like a dreamer's, will be left indelibly marked. So intense is this new value, and, at the same time, so strongly forbidden is its nature, that it is not only displaced onto these relatively minor figures but it is further concealed by being displaced into the innocent game of cribbage that they play. The result is that cribbage always afterwards carries connotations of sexual intercourse in Dickens' novels.

The work of analysis in a case such as this has some of the same quality as teasing out the solution of a cryptogram. The author's or dreamer's mind which is telling the story wants desperately to express certain feelings; he does not want the precise reference of those feelings to be explicitly understood. It is important to remember that the evidence our analysis seeks will not all hang together with logical consistency, because it is not with logic that this part of the mind works. We must take each piece of evidence separately. It is their reiteration as separate bits that reinforces their collective significance even while they conflict with or contradict one another.

We need also remember that in the realm of the unconscious mind where dreams are made there are no neat compartments. All of the meaning in all of the dreams tends to be linked together in a vast and tangled network. It is not possible to begin to analyze the various associations of one of Dickens' props without getting drawn into more and more of the associations of the other props. Such compartmentalization and limitation as I have imposed here for the convenience of presentation is to some degree arbitrary and tends to belie the material it seeks to reveal.

It is like unravelling a sweater. At whatever point in the garment the first loose end of the yarn appears, the whole must be dismembered before one comes to the end of the thread.

In seeking to discover the source of the psychic intensity expressed in Dick Swiveller and the Marchioness while engaged in their favorite game, it is useful to try to identify them, to determine *who they are*. We know more or less who Dick is. At least it appears to us that we do. But we know very little about the Marchioness. Dick himself is curious about this, and before the end of the novel he strongly suspects that he knows who she is.

> Mr. Brass had said once, that he believed she was a "love-child" (which means anything but a child of love), and that was all the information Richard Swiveller could obtain.

There is no reason to suppose Sampson knows more about the Marchioness' identity than, say, Squire Allworthy knew about the identity of Tom Jones. Sampson may, however, actually know more than he is saying. Indeed, on the occasion of the general confession of his guilty knowledge he hints as much. At all events Richard remains curious about the girl and when Sally Brass goes off to dinner he followed her

> with his eyes to the door, and with his ears to a little back parlour, where she and her brother took their meals.
> "Now," said Dick, walking up and down with his hands in his pockets, "I'd give something—if I had it—to know how they use that child, and where they keep her. My mother must have been a very inquisitive woman; I have no doubt I'm marked with a note of interrogation some-

where. My feelings I smother, but thou hast been the cause of this anguish, my—upon my word," said Mr. Swiveller, checking himself, and falling thoughtfully into the client's chair, "I should like to know how they use her!"

In this circular monologue which begins and ends with an inquiry about how the Brasses behave toward the little girl, it is evident that an illumination of some sort has occurred to frustrate the consummation of the rhyme of what is a bit of comic doggerel. It is at the point where Dick's rambling verse breaks off that there first begins to dawn in his mind an idea of the identity of the person who may possibly have fulfilled for the Marchioness the role referred to by the word, "Mother," which he omits. Indeed, that is why he omits it and why the inquiry acquires the enigmatically circular nature it has. The word, "Mother," itself starts an illuminating train of thought which Dick is not yet prepared to put into words.

Dick proceeds to spy upon Sally Brass feeding the little servant and then, at the conclusion of the chapter, observes Miss Brass' unaccountable and apparently gratuitous sadism toward the little girl.

It was plain that some extraordinary grudge was working in Miss Brass' gentle breast, and that it was this which impelled her, without the smallest present cause, to rap the child with the blade of the knife, now on her hand, now on her head, and now on her back, as if she found it quite impossible to stand so close to her without administering a few slight knocks. But Mr. Swiveller was not a little surprised to see his fellow clerk, after walking slowly backwards towards the door, as if she were trying to withdraw herself from the room but could not accomplish it, dart suddenly forward, and falling on the small servant give her some hard blows with her clenched hand.

The hostility is so strong it is evident Miss Brass actually hates the existence of this, her illegitimate child, as Dick clearly suspects her to be, although neither he nor anyone else in the novel ever says so in so many words. Dick makes this suspicion further clear to us through what is again an interesting verbal association, significantly a punning bit of verbal wit.

"What's the matter?" said the dwarf, advancing. "Has Sally proved unkind? 'Of all the girls that are so smart, there's none like—' eh, Dick!"
"Certainly not," replied Mr. Swiveller, eating his dinner with great gravity, "none like her. She's the sphynx of private life is Sally B."

Daniel Quilp evidently shares Dick's knowledge of popular comic songs and further shares his propensity for alluding to delicate matters by means of partially incomplete verses. Having referred to the mother as a sphinx, Dick later, when he becomes the daughter's guardian, use the same word for her.

After casting about for some time for a name which should be worthy of her [the Marchioness], he [Dick Swiveller] decided in favour of Sophronia Sphynx, as being euphonious and genteel, and furthermore indicative of mystery.

It often happens that a child born out of wedlock will be given her mother's maiden name for lack of a father's name to give her. But what is more important to us, such a

close verbal association could not possibly occur in Dick's
mind, or in Dickens', accidentally.

Dick has a strong suspicion about her father too. When
Quilp calls at Bevis Marks to invite the Brasses to his
little tea-party at the Wilderness to plot the criminal conspiracy against Christopher Nubbles, he conducts a very
interesting interview with the little servant.

> "Eh?" said the dwarf, looking down (it was something
> quite new to him) upon the small servant.

There are not very many families of dwarfs. There are
very few people small enough for Quilp to look down upon.
The Brasses are both out, and Quilp writes them a note.

> As Mr. Quilp folded his note (which was soon written:
> being a very short one) he encountered the gaze of the
> small servant. He looked at her long and earnestly.

He frightens her, as he does many people. The line of
inquiry he takes is the same one which first occurred to
Mr. Swiveller in connection with her.

> "Do they use you ill here? is your mistress a Tartar?"
> said Quilp with a chuckle.
> In reply to the last interrogation, the small servant, with
> a look of infinite cunning mingled with fear, screwed up
> her mouth very tight and round, and nodded violently.
> Whether there was anything in the peculiar slyness of
> her action which fascinated Mr. Quilp, or anything in the
> expression of her features at the moment which attracted
> his attention for some other reason; or whether it merely
> occurred to him as a pleasant whim to stare the small
> servant out of countenance; certain it is, that he planted

his elbows square and firmly on the desk, and squeezing up his cheeks with his hands, looked at her fixedly.

"Where do you come from?" He said after a long pause, stroking his chin.

"I don't know."

"What's your name?"

"Nothing."

"Nonsense!" retorted Quilp. "What does your mistress call you when she wants you?"

"A little devil," said the child.

At this point Quilp's own mind is evidently satisfied.

These unusual answers might naturally have provoked some more inquiries. Quilp, however, without uttering another word, withdrew his eyes from the small servant, stroked his chin more thoughtfully than before, and then, bending over the note as if to direct it with scrupulous and hairbreadth nicety, looked at her, covertly but very narrowly, from under his bushy eyebrows. The result of this secret survey was, that he shaded his face with his hands, and laughed slyly and noiselessly, until every vein in it was swollen almost to bursting. Pulling his hat over his brow to conceal his mirth and its effects, he tossed the letter to the child, and hastily withdrew.

Once in the street, moved by some secret impulse, he laughed, and held his sides, and laughed again, and tried to peer through the dusty area railings as if to catch another glimpse of the child, until he was quite tired out.

Quilp's reflections are quite clear. He had almost forgotten that brief sexual encounter with Sally Brass. Goblinlike in many ways, Quilp's rapaciousness is not limited to money matters. Although his orientation is primarily sadistic, Quilp is a prodigy of every kind of sexual energy. While Sally's moustache and other dubious charms might repel lesser creatures, Quilp will ecstatically rape anyone who gives him the most trifling excuse to drop his only just barely maintained restraints. But from that fantastic union Quilp had not until now realized there had been issue. They are, indeed, a family.

And, by the end of the book, the guilty secret Quilp and Sally share is known to Dick Swiveller.

> Mr. Swiveller, having always been in some measure of a philosophic and reflective turn, grew immensely contemplative, at times, in the smoking-box, and was accustomed at such periods to debate in his own mind the mysterious question of Sophronia's parentage. Sophronia herself supposed she was an orphan; but Mr. Swiveller, putting various slight circumstances together, often thought Miss Brass must know better than that; and, having heard from his wife of her strange interview with Quilp, entertained sundry misgivings whether that person, in his lifetime, might not also have been able to solve the riddle, had he chosen. These speculations, however, gave him no uneasiness. . . .

It would, clearly, have been the riddle of the "Sphynx" to which Quilp had the solution, rendering him a kind of comic Oedipus who gets away with it. At all events, since Dick is a wise husband, he does not blame his wife for his in-laws, especially since he never has to see them, anyway.

Now that it is clear that Dick Swiveller married the illegitimate daughter of Daniel Quilp and Sally Brass, it is possible to proceed to the more important functions and relationships Dick and the Marchioness express by displacement for other persons in this dream-like drama. One of the most important of these is that Dick represents Quilp as well as himself.

Dick is the Marchioness' father too. This renders him,

too, a kind of comic Oedipus whose children were his brothers and sisters. He actually brings the small servant out of the underground cave in which she has only had a kind of nonexistence, or pre-existence, up to that point, and introduces her to life. He gives her the only names, apparently, that she has ever had. He feeds her, and later, clothes her. She is his ward for a time. He is responsible for her nurture and education. He stands to her, indeed, *in loco parentis*. He thus represents Quilp, her father by blood, and is one of the first of several men in Dickens' novels who fall in love with their daughters. He differs from some of the others in that he does really marry her, and consummates the union—at least symbolically—many hundred thousand times.

It is indeed the case that when Quilp first introduces Dick Swiveller to Sampson and Sally Brass he hands on his quondam paramour lasciviously, as it were, to Dick.

> "Is that my Sally?" croaked the dwarf, ogling the fair Miss Brass. "Is it Justice with the bandage off her eyes, and without the sword and scales? Is it the Strong Arm of the Law? Is it the Virgin of Bevis?"

And as soon as he brings Dick in through the door he continues:

> "There she is," said Quilp, stopping short at the door, and wrinkling up his eyebrows as he looked towards Miss Sally; "there is the woman I ought to have married—there is the beautiful Sarah—there is the female who has all the charms of her sex and none of their weaknesses. Oh Sally, Sally!"

A good part of the humor of it, of course, is that there is

more truth to it than there appears to be. The best kind of lie is the truth told so it won't be believed. Before he concludes the introduction, Quilp gives Dick and Sally together his blessings:

> "Miss Sally will teach him law, the delightful study of the law," said Quilp; "she'll be his guide, his friend, his companion, his Blackstone, his Coke upon Littleton, his Young Lawyer's Best Companion."

And the truth of the matter is that Dick "found favour in the eyes of Miss Sally Brass." Not in the way Quilp had done, of course. The affair is far more platonic and is mainly limited to amusements of a social rather than a sexual sort. Nevertheless, in his own way Dick succeeds Quilp with Sally and upon her he "burst in full freshness as something new and hitherto undreamed of . . ."

Again, and in a quite different way, Dick is further identified with Quilp because Quilp is *his* father too. The first time Quilp gets Dick drunk there is the memorable scene in which Dick bewails his orphan lot.

> "Here," said Mr. Swiveller, raising his voice to a high pitch, and looking sleepily round, "is a miserable orphan!"
>
> "Then," said someone hard by, "let me be a father to you."
>
> Mr. Swiveller swayed himself to and fro to preserve his balance, and, looking into a kind of haze which seemed to surround him, at last perceived two eyes dimly twinkling through the mist, which he observed after a short time were in the neighbourhood of a nose and mouth. Casting his eyes down towards that quarter in which, with reference to a man's face, his legs are usually to be found, he observed that the face had a body attached. . . .

Dick's inebriation renders this perception a kind of fantasy, almost a dream. As we shall observe, it is in dreams within dreams, like this dream within the novel, that the deepest layers of psychic meaning are to be encountered.

The correspondence between the upper and lower parts of the body which occur widely throughout dreams, folklore, and wit, relates the upper cheeks to the lower ones, the lips to the labia, the nose to the penis, facial hair to pubic hair, and the eyes to testicles. On a number of significant, crucial occasions through the novels we shall discover that the father appears symbolically represented by his genitals. In view especially of the location in which they are described, it is evident that Dick is looking at the progenitive organs which brought him into being, and which he discovers are "hard" by.

> "You have deceived an orphan, sir," said Mr. Swiveller solemnly.
> "I! I'm a second father to you," replied Quilp.

With the realization that Quilp is also Little Nell's father, or rather, an alter ego for her grandfather, we begin to come close to the source of the psychic intensities displaced upon Dick and the Marchioness. It is difficult, perhaps, to see Quilp in the trembling, fearful old man who is led through the wilderness by the child. But when his mania is upon him, when he gambles with Isaac List and Jowl, then it is possible to see Quilp's rapacity peering out through his eyes. When the apparition comes creeping into Nell's bedroom to steal their last supply of money for his gambling, it is almost as if it were the same apparition of Quilp that Nell fears to see among Mrs. Jarley's waxwork figures, and which she does indeed see coming through the old gate with its other gargoyles in niches. It is Quilp and

Grandfather Trent *together* who in their complementary ways hunt and haunt and hound Nell to her destruction.

There is thus more meaning to Quilp's putting Dick Swiveller up to the expectation of marrying Little Nell than his mere apparent desire to trick him and Fred Trent. For Dick stands for Quilp himself, and it is really Quilp who wants to put himself in the place where he pretends to place his surrogate, Dick Swiveller. In his pursuit of the Trents, Quilp is after more than just the money he can make out of them. He had earlier suggested to Nell that she might in a few years become his second wife, "my little cherry-cheeked, red lipped wife."

When Quilp takes over the Old Curiosity Shop because of Grandfather Trent's indebtedness to him, the first thing he usurps is Nell's little bed to lie in. Her last moments of terror in the shop before they flee London for the country involve Nell in the bizarre horror of sneaking past Quilp grotesquely, obscenely, frighteningly asleep in her bed. When Nell finally escapes into death from the wickedness of the world it is from a fate worse than death that she is escaping. Dick Swiveller himself dimly sees that the Marchioness stands for Nell even in his own terms, because after the Marchioness marries him, Dick had "frequent occasion to remark at divers subsequent periods that there had been a young lady saving up for him after all."

The final unravelling of the identities which lie behind Dick and the Marchioness brings us at last to Charles Dickens himself. There is, of course, something of an author in every one of his characters. But there is more of Dickens in some characters than in others, and what is most important to determine is what part of the author may be found in which characters. We shall, at any rate, have opportunities to observe that Dickens tends to feel a special interest in and sympathy for characters, especially

young men, who exhibit a high level of verbal wit. He also
tends to be identified in special ways with characters whose
names involve a form of his own name, or a play on his
own name, or even on his initials. Further, Dickens indicated to his friend John Forster that in Daniel Quilp's
sadistic behavior toward his mother-in-law, Mrs. Jiniwin,
there was a comic expression of some of his own feelings
about his own mother-in-law.

When Dickens married Catherine Hogarth her younger
sister, Mary, came to live with the young couple. Dickens
thus began married life with two admiring young women.
In some ways the pretty, vivacious, intelligent younger
sister idolized the handsome young genius even more than
his wife did. At the age of seventeen Mary Hogarth died
suddenly and utterly unexpectedly in her brother-in-law's
arms. The shock to Dickens was profound, its effects life-
long. Her memory came to represent for him all that was
good and pure in the world, and that died young. It is
quite clear that in creating the story of Little Nell and her
death Dickens was reliving for himself, and in a displaced,
symbolic way for the whole world, the complexities of his
thoughts and feelings about Mary Hogarth.

It would be much too simple, and simply too wrong to
suggest that Charles Dickens entertained in any conscious
way for his sister-in-law the kinds of feelings Daniel Quilp
had for Ellen Trent. On the other hand, it is likely he perceived that she was attractive. At the deepest unconscious
level of irrational infantile thought, the level where dreams
and great works of art are produced, it is entirely possible
for a strong desire regarded as wicked to be considered
guilty for anything bad which happens to its object. The
hateful desire for the pure girl could, at that level, be *felt*
to have murdered her. There is a bit of Daniel Quilp in
everyone. The character, like so many of Dickens' char-

acters, has a universal appeal. But few people in ordinary life are forced to confront the bit of Quilp in themselves with the *fact* of the sudden and otherwise inexplicable death of someone toward whom they may have momentarily entertained Quilplike feelings. Dickens' psyche as a man, as a Victorian, and as an artist polarized everything erotic as being wicked, and everything altruistic, caritative and self-sacrificing as being wholly good. Erotic love and caritative love were poles apart and, indeed, *could not be permitted* to come together because the one which represented all evil would destroy the one which represented the world's only good. The struggle between the good one and the bad one, and the ultimate transformation and redemption of the bad one by the good one, constitutes a major theme underlying all of Dickens' creative work. We shall pursue the unravelling of it throughout this book.

It is unthinkable for the satyr Quilp to accomplish the violation of the pure child. It is unthinkable for the father, Quilp with his alter ego Grandfather Trent, actually to violate the daughter-like figure. It is unthinkable for the brother, Quilp with his son and surrogate Swiveller, to violate the sister-like figure. But the desire to do so is tremendous and it is there. It has to go somewhere. The wish in some way has to be fulfilled. And Dick Swiveller and the Marchioness playing cribbage together provide a suitably disguised way for that desire to express itself, to get past the censor. That is why they play so many hundred thousand games and why the game consistently maintains its sexual connotation throughout the rest of the novels.

The fact is, of course, that the whole and wholly sane psyche needs to feel and to express both kinds of love, both the erotic and the caritative, both the love which creates and the love which cares and nurtures. The struggle to reconcile the two, to bring the two together in a healthy union goes on throughout Dickens' novel writing career. It constitutes one of the major themes of that unconscious, largely sexual mythology which evolves through the associations which attach to the props.

Here at the early stage in Dickens' career at which the *Old Curiosity Shop* was written, it is quite intolerable to consider even for a moment that *eros* and *caritas,* that Quilp and Nell, might be permitted to come together. Toward the close of Dickens' career, in the last novel he completed, *Our Mutual Friend,* that union is, as we shall see, finally brought about.

Even here at the early stage of his career one can see a foreshadowing of the fact that the ideal soul who is Little Nell is a part of the same total *person* at the other end of whose continuum of urges and feelings is the evil devil Quilp. The Marchioness is, after all, Quilp's child, his own flesh and blood. And she comes to stand for the pure young girl. But at the same time she can be married, and she can play cribbage.

Chapter II

THE WINGS OF HIS MIND

The Erotic Meaning of Wooden Legs

THIS CHAPTER, and the two following it, will be devoted to the dream interpretation of the very large number of sexual symbols and images in Dickens' novels. The organization of these chapters will reveal still another respect in which these novels resemble dreams. That is the tendency of a series of dreams dreamt by the same dreamer, especially when dreamt in the same night, to reveal their central, unifying themes more and more explicitly and candidly as the series progresses. Meaning deeply buried, cryptographically concealed, and rigidly censored in the early versions of the dreams will become, in the later ones, quite evident and transparent. Dickens' novels clearly operate on some very similar principle. What is merely hinted at in *Pickwick* becomes a central and explicit theme in *Little Dorrit,* or even in *Barnaby Rudge;* what is only suggested in the *Old Curi-*

osity Shop or in *David Copperfield* becomes flagrantly overt in *Our Mutual Friend* or in *Edwin Drood*.

There is much in the novels and there will be much in the following pages to illustrate this characteristic of Dickens' fiction. For purposes of illustration at this point it may suffice to mention shoemaking. Shoemakers are skilled artisans, on the one hand, but on the other, it is, after all, *shoes* that they make, shoes that are indelibly stained with shoeblacking. It is getting a bit ahead of ourselves to mention it here, but shoemakers in Dickens' novels are invariably father figures of one sort or another. The shoes on which they tap, tap, tap often figure symbolically in dream and folk lore as representative of the female genital organ. Vulva tapping, as we have already seen, is often regarded as a discreditable activity.

Since the series of Dickens' novels seem to behave like a series of dreams, we shall often have occasion to turn to *Pickwick* for the earliest statement of a major theme which runs through all of the novels. That is where we find the nuclear, archetypal shoemaker. Among the many other sorts and conditions of men Mr. Pickwick meets when he is imprisoned for debt is the Chancery prisoner, who is dying, and who has been imprisoned there for ever so long.

He was a sallow man—all cobblers are; and had a strong bristly beard—all cobblers have. His face was a queer, good-tempered, crooked-featured piece of workmanship, ornamented with a couple of eyes that must have worn a very joyous expression at one time, for they sparkled yet. The man was sixty, by years, and Heaven knows how old by imprisonment, so that his having any look approaching to mirth or contentment was singular enough. He was a little man, and, being half doubled up as he lay in bed, looked about as long as he ought to

have been without his legs. He had a great red pipe in
his mouth, and was smoking, and staring at the rush-light,
in a state of enviable placidity.

Here is a clear association, that is, simultaneity of occurrence, between shoemaking and punishment. A bit later in
this chapter we shall see that added to the punishment of
his being in prison there is the additional punishment of
his *apparently* being without legs. We need not wonder
too much about what this man's guilt may be, that he
should be so punished. We can understand it well enough
when we next encounter precisely this scene, for then it is
dwarf Daniel Quilp smoking his pipe as he lies in Little
Nell's bed. Father figures who are like babies, either as to
size or as to the kind of care they require from the caritative loving figure, become a major theme in Dickens'
novels. One feels great compassion for these father figures
in prison, because prisons are like death. And of course
young Charles Dickens never forgot the terrible suffering
associated with his father's imprisonment for debt.

In *Nicholas Nickleby,* when educator Squeers is finally
imprisoned and wants to express the notion that he has
come to the end of his wretched career, he puts it this way:

> . . . this is an altered state of trigonomics, this is! A double
> 1—all, everything—a cobbler's weapon. U-p—up, adjec-
> tive, not down. S-q-u double e-r-s—Squeers, noun sub-
> stantive, a educator of youth. Total, all up with Squeers!

The "cobbler's weapon," of course, is the *awl,* a pointed
tool for making holes in wood or leather. But if you take
just what he spells, with the definitions he uses, you get a
singularly vicious and obscene form of punishment. It is,
indeed, a shoemaker's "Up yours!"

One of Mr. Micawber's detaining creditors in *David Copperfield* when he goes to prison for debt is a "dirty-faced man (I think he was a boot-maker). . . ." Elements of Mr. Pickwick's prisoner appear in *Bleak House,* which is all about Chancery, and in *Little Dorrit,* which is all about imprisonment for debt and which details the motherly care given to a childlike father by a devoted, pure daughter, Little Dorrit, whose very name bespeaks her kinship with Little Nell.

It is of course absolutely wrong for the wicked father figure to seek erotic union with the ideal girl child, but it is perfectly praiseworthy for her to seek to give him all the loving *care* he so desperately needs despite the fact that he certainly does not deserve it. In the profound urge to bring these two figures together in one healthy union (which is, of course, much deeper than any merely sexual yen, however strong, the older man may have for the younger girl) this permissible act of the idealized member of the pair to move toward the other, wicked member, is a first, major step toward their ultimate union.

The most important occurrence of imprisoned shoemaking in the later novels is that of Alexandre Manette, the Doctor of Beauvais, in *A Tale of Two Cities,* who learned the craft while entombed in the Bastille, and for whom the *activity* of shoemaking remains the primary symptom of his recurring psychological and spiritual imprisonment. It has become his way of dealing with a sense of imprisonment. We may observe the association coming back, full circle, when Jarvis Lorry discusses the hypothetical problem of the man who relapsed into a certain occupation, in order to get Manette to consider his own case objectively and professionally: "the occupation resumed," said Mr. Lorry, clearing his throat, "we will call—Blacksmith's work, Blacksmith's work." Here is another clear line established from shoemaking to blacksmithing. It underscores the fact that Pip working for Joe Gargery at the forge is tantamount to David Copperfield working for Murdstone and Grinby. "I was truly wretched, and had a strong conviction on me that I should never like Joe's trade."

Furthermore in *Great Expectations* it is with his blacksmith's hammer that Dolge Orlick anticipates killing Pip, and it is almost certainly with such a hammer that he assaulted and crippled Pip's sister, Mrs. Joe Gargery, an act to which we shall again refer in the fifth chapter.

In this novel blacksmithing and imprisonment are kept separate in the two persons of Joe Gargery and Abel Magwitch. The two are united symbolically in their relationships to the central figure because each of these two men fills for Pip, in different ways, the role of father. The point is that the associative simultaneity of shoemaking and punishment gets larger and more prominent as we proceed through the novels, rather like a snowball rolling downhill, or, like the meaning of a series of related dreams.

In much the same way the snowball made by the increasingly explicit sexual connotations of a number of the props reaches its maximum dimensions in *Our Mutual Friend*, the last novel Dickens completed. As we shall see, there are indications that certain of the props might have achieved even greater prominence in *Edwin Drood* had that book been finished. It is certain that what might be called the sexual mythology which environs the props and endows them with meaning would have taken further major steps in its unfolding in *Drood*. But for our purposes here the most emphatic occurrence of the largest number of sexual props takes place in this culminating novel on the occasion of the wedding of the central figure, John Harmon. He is "our mutual friend" to the Boffins and Wilfers. When John Harmon, still using the name Rokesmith, marries Bella Wilfer, the passage describing the event becomes so singularly intense, ecstatic, and visionary as to be virtually dreamlike. It is like a dream within a dream, and the consequently extraordinary intensity is such that one should expect analysis to reveal the most varied and extensive meaning.

By examining each prop which appears on this occasion, each fragment of the scene in turn, we can trace the prop's sexual connotations up through the novels. We can thus unravel the far-reaching trains of thought and meaning which come to bear upon Bella and John Harmon, and in and through them illuminate the whole mythology of essentially sexual meaning which runs through and underlies all of Dickens' novels.

We might well begin with wooden legs. There was a wooden-legged man at Florence Dombey's wedding in *Dombey and Son* who "pegs his way among the echoes out of doors." There is a wooden-legged man at Bella Wilfer's wedding in *Our Mutual Friend* as well, and, he too "pegged away as if he were scoring furiously at cribbage." If there were nothing else to point toward hidden meaning in the text, that would do it. It is hidden meaning which seems clearly associated with a wooden-legged man. *Our Mutual Friend* is, indeed, the novel with a major character who has a wooden leg, Silas Wegg. And Wegg is, as a matter of fact, associated in a curious way with the earliest master cribbage scorer, Dick Swiveller. Both Wegg and Swiveller are "literary" men who "drop" frequently into verse. The difference is that Swiveller's verse is usually the better of the two.

> Yet loved I as man never loved that hadn't wooden legs, and my heart, my heart is breaking for the love of Sophy Cheggs.

Another comic song, and here Wegg's name comes very close to rhyming with Cheggs. He is, furthermore, well on his way toward having *two* wooden legs. This circumstance is rendered interesting by the fact that old Gruff and Glum, the wooden-legged man at Bella Wilfer's wedding, has two wooden legs. Silas Wegg has told Mr. Boffin that he got his wooden leg in an accident, and it is especially thrilling to Noddy Boffin that he will have a literary man, *with* a wooden leg. Mr. Wegg is altogether such a wooden man

> that he seemed to have taken his wooden leg naturally, and rather suggested to the fanciful observer, that he might be expected—if his development received no untimely check—to be completely set up with a pair of wooden legs in about six months.

Even though a good deal more time than six months elapses between Silas Wegg's advent here, at the opening of the novel, and Gruff and Glum's appearance toward its end, we shall discover that symbolically old Gruff and Glum represents the same person, the same relationship, as does Silas Wegg.

A wooden leg signifies, on the one hand, that a real flesh and blood leg has been cut off. On the other hand, it is a more rigid member than that which it replaces. It is an example of the way in which the unconscious ideation which produces dreams unites opposite meanings in a single image. A wooden leg represents simultaneously a castration and the rigid phallus that has been cut off. In either event it is not an accident that Wegg enlists the aid of a man with the name of the goddess of love to seek for the bones of the leg he lost.

> Mr. Venus takes from a corner by his chair, the bones

of a leg and foot, beautifully pure, and put together with exquisite neatness. These he compares with Mr. Wegg's leg; that gentleman looking on, as if he were being measured for a riding boot.

"You have got a twist in that bone, to the best of my belief."

Like old Gruff and Glum, Wegg thinks a lot about that missing leg. We learn about the former that

for years the wings of his mind had gone to look after the legs of his body; but Bella had brought them back for him per steamer, and they were spread again.

The wings of Wegg's mind have gone to look after the leg of his body, too, but the difference is that he has Venus' aid. Bella brings back to old Gruff and Glum only the wings of his mind, that had been looking for his legs. But Venus actually succeeds in returning Wegg's leg's bones to him in a brown paper parcel.

Old Gruff and Glum can only manage what seems comically to symbolize a proximate erection "with his wooden legs horizontally disposed before him." But Silas Wegg can do much better. When he first reads the lives of the misers to the Golden Dustman the slightly displaced erotic excitement caused by reading what is, after all, a kind of fiscal pornography, is so great that Wegg's wooden leg "started forward under the table, and slowly elevated itself as he read on" getting further and further up until the hilarious pseudo-erection unbalances him and he falls over on to Venus, mounts Venus, in fact.

The identities hidden behind Wegg and Venus are naturally of considerable importance in determining their sexual significance. As we saw with Richard Swiveller and the

Marchioness, the unravelling of just who the character is leads one to the core of sexual meaning embodied in the character's functions and relationships. The business of these chapters, then, will consist in a large degree in the determining of the hidden identities of a number of key characters.

We can take a first step toward the discovery of Wegg's hidden identity by examining the occurrence of his wooden erection in other places in the novels. In *Great Expectations,* Pip's one direct, existential perception of old Bill Barley, Herbert Pocket's father-in-law to be, is of a loud noise, a growl in the beam:

> the growl swelled into a roar again, and a frightful bumping noise was heard above, as if a giant with a wooden leg were trying to bore it through the ceiling to come at us.

When we reflect that rooms in dreams often represent the woman, the image begins to clear and to make more sense. This scene is an unconscious fantasy that is set *in utero.* The giant is the father, the room the mother. It is another genital encounter with the father. It is the progenitive phallus that threatens to come at us, prenatally. It is the phallus of the man who has to die before we can have the pretty girl for a wife (and Herbert does have to wait for that event before his marriage). It is the phallus of the man who not only controls the girl but the food as well (and Mr. Barley does nightly dole out his own and his daughter's rations).

This is the situation with Barley in *Great Expectations,* and it is the situation with Bray in *Nicholas Nickleby.* It is Madeline Bray's father who conspires with Ralph Nickleby to sell her to Arthur Gride. Nicholas cannot get at her to

woo her and marry her until Madeline's father dies and re-
leases her from Uncle Ralph's and Arthur Gride's power.
And Nicholas' exact existential perception of Mr. Bray's
death is important and relates to Pip's and Herbert's experience of Bill Barley.

> Ralph, being by this time as furious as a baffled tiger,
> made for the door, and, attempting to pass Kate, clasped
> her arm roughly with his hand. Nicholas, with his eyes
> darting fire, seized him by the collar. At that moment,
> a heavy body fell with great violence on the floor above,
> and, in an instant afterwards, was heard a most appalling
> and terrific scream.

The instructive detail, of course, is that loud bumping
noise upstairs. There are other suggestive details here.
Nicholas is struggling with Ralph in order to protect Kate.
Simultaneously upstairs Bray falls down dead with a loud
bang and frees Madeline for Nicholas. The older men are
multiple versions of each other, and the girls are multiple
versions of each other.

In the network of sexual meaning in *Nicholas Nickleby,*
Uncle Ralph and Mr. Bray are not really to be distinguished from one another, nor is Kate to be found really
distinct from Madeline. The unconscious sexual mythology
underlying the novel is one in which sons struggle with
their fathers for the girls and other valuables which their
fathers possess. Nicholas and Smike and Frank Cheeryble
represent the sons; Ralph and Bray and Gride (and
Squeers) represent the fathers. (The Cheeryble brothers
represent the good, beneficent side of the father.) Kate
and Madeline represent the girls. These are matters which
will be discussed more fully later. They illustrate how diffi-

cult it is to discuss any *one* aspect of the unconscious sexual ideation underlying the novels without discussing *all* aspects of it at the same time.

For the moment, however, I want to pursue Bill Barley and Mr. Bray a little further and to include Mr. Barkis. When David Copperfield visits ailing Barkis' bedside he observes that

> his right hand came slowly and feebly from under the bedclothes, and with a purposeless uncertain grasp took hold of a stick which was loosely tied to the side of the bed. After some poking about with this instrument, in the course of which his face assumed a variety of distracted expressions, Mr. Barkis poked it against a box, an end of which had been visible to me all the time. Then his face became composed.

"Old clothes," said Mr. Barkis. Boxes, cases, chests, receptacles of all sorts serve in dreams as rooms do, except that they are more likely to be specific, especially when they are under beds and partly revealed and partly hidden, and mean not the whole woman, but just her genitals. Aside from this slight difference, and the fact that it is a stick rather than a wooden leg, it is clear that the fantasy adumbrated here in a comically symbolic way is that of an act of coition. Mr. Barkis does not, like Barley and Bray, apparently have control of a pretty girl he's keeping away from the principal self who is, in this novel, David Copperfield. But he does control the food, and that is inside the box, in the form of money. He wants Clara Peggotty Barkis to feed David and Steerforth well:

> "My dear, you'll get a dinner to-day for company— something good to eat and drink will you?"

But in order to enable her to do so he has to get some money for her from the precious box, without, of course, letting on that is where it comes from. He pretends to need a nap.

> When we got outside the door, Peggotty informed me that Mr. Barkis, being now a "little nearer" than he used to be, always resorted to this same device before producing a single coin from his store; and that he endured unheard-of agonies in crawling out of bed alone, and taking it from that unlucky box. In effect, we presently heard him uttering suppressed groans of the most dismal nature, as this magpie proceeding wracked him in every joint.

This is clearly another displaced and comic version of that same act of coition. This time it is not directly seen, but only overheard.

> So he groaned on, until he got into bed again, suffering, I have no doubt, a martyrdom; and then called us in, pretending to have just woke up from a refreshing sleep, and to produce a guinea from under his pillow. His satisfaction in which happy imposition on us, and in having preserved the impenetrable secret of the box, appeared to be a sufficient compensation to him for all his tortures.

It is a symbolic, aural version of the primal scene, which Dickens sees as the self-progenitive act of sexual intercourse between the child's parents. It is the time when he was begot. It first appears in Dickens' novels when Oliver Twist, half awake and half asleep, observes Fagin playing with the golden trinkets he takes from the box he took from the secret hole.

Even when he is on the point of death Barkis still makes evident his devotion to the precious box.

He was lying with his head and shoulders out of bed, in an uncomfortable attitude, half resting on the box which had cost him so much pain and trouble. I learned that, when he was past creeping out of bed to open it, and past assuring himself of its safety by means of the divining rod I had seen him use, he had required to have it placed on the chair at the bedside, where he had ever since embraced it, night and day. His arm lay on it now.

There is an evident three-way association of gold with food and girls. We will not completely unravel it until we come to the fourth chapter. At the present moment we may remark that Mr. Barkis is somewhere between Mr. Bray and Mr. Barley. Mr. Bray controls the girl, but not the food. Mr. Barkis controls the food, but not the girl. In his case there does not appear to be a girl. Even these slight distinctions are instructive, Mr. Barkis' lack of a pretty girl especially so. Old Bill Barley, of course, controls the food and the girl.

Mr. Barkis doesn't have a pretty girl to deprive David of, but he *is* married to Clara Peggotty, whose first name is the same as David's mother's. She is one of David's primary mother-surrogates in the novel, and lived with David's young girl mother in the pre-Murdstone Garden of Eden. We shall have occasion to perceive that there is a whole category of young, pretty girls in the novels who are a displaced version of one aspect of the mother figure.

The pathway through the sexual mythology of the novels is not a straight one. It is useful here, in the pursuit of the meaning of wooden legs, to make a long digression from

them to mention two bits of folklore which are prominent
in that sexual mythology and which therefore have to be
brought explicitly into the discussion sooner or later. One
is the tale of the Loathly Hag, the other the story of Jack
and the Beanstalk. Both of these tales in virtually all of
their versions relate to the oedipal situation, from different
points of view, and both are intimately woven into
Dickens' unconscious sexual mythology.

The Loathly Hag is a repulsive woman who possesses
magical powers and superhuman wisdom or knowledge.
She almost always appears in close conjunction with a
young, pretty, sexually desirable girl. Very often she transforms herself into the young and sexually desirable girl.
This sometimes happens after she has forced the despondent
knight to marry her and has in fact gotten into bed with
him. In order to break the spell and transform her into
the ruddy young desirable girl, either a question must be
answered, a riddle solved, or some other magic formula
applied. Oedipus' riddle of the sphinx is a special case of
this action.

The unconscious mind of the young boy, who is in
love with his mother, breaks up his own ambivalence of
feeling about her into two separate entities. One is the
memory of the young mother of early childhood. She is the
young girl upon whom the sexual desire can safely be
fastened. This is partly because his desire began as a child
before he had to repress his feelings towards her, and partly
because the image of that beautiful girl does not resemble the present appearance of the mother. The difference is not really one of years so much as it is a
difference in the child's two attitudes. The mother he saw
as a divine young love goddess looks very different from
the image of the mother which he saw after his desire
for her is repressed. The actual lapse of time is not so great

as to account for such physical changes in his mother. That the present image of the mother is not only not sexually attractive but is sexually repulsive is due mainly to repression. The stronger the unconscious sexual desire for the young girl mother, the more intense the loathesomeness of the old hag mother. The very fact that they are polar opposites helps protect the psyche from facing the realization that they are the same person. It is analogous to the separation we have already seen between Daniel Quilp and Little Nell. It is symptomatic of the divorce in the earlier novels between erotic love and caritative love.

Clara Peggotty and Clara Cooperfield are just such a single person, differentiated from one another just sufficiently to protect young David's psyche from the realization of their identity in his pre-Murdstone Garden of Eden. It would be cruelly unkind to Clara Peggotty (and a bit of a slur on Mr. Barkis, too) to say that she was loathly. But it was Clara Copperfield who was the erotic love object, the "dolly," as Aunt Betsey Trotwood so accurately observed. The caritative functions of motherhood were mainly reserved for Peggotty. Because the dichotomy of persons is only apparent and not real in terms of the actual relationships symbolized, it becomes clear that Mr. Barkis did have control of a pretty girl after all, at least by displacement, as well as having control of the food. We shall often find it instructive to look in the sexual network of a Dickens novel for the two persons who embody the two aspects of the Loathly Hag.

It is up an enormously phallic Beanstalk, the biggest erection in the world, that Jack must climb in order to steal things from the giant. While up at its top he meets the not unfriendly but equally large giantess who is the giant's wife. She protects Jack from the giant by hiding him in her uterus (she really is the mother, after all) that is, in the oven or in the woodbox. When Jack cuts down the tremendously phallic Beanstalk he simultaneously kills the giant. It is quite clear the giant is the father, the giantess the mother, and that Jack is involved in rivalry with the former for favors from the latter.

Part of the situation with Messrs. Bray, Barkis and Barley is that they are *upstairs.* Indeed, Pip's surrogate father Abel Magwitch is on the third floor up above Bill Barley. Barley is on the second floor directly over the parlor in which Pip and Herbert are sitting when they hear the growl in the beam which sounded so like a giant with a gigantic wooden leg. The situation is further enriched by the fact that Abel Magwitch is not only Pip's surrogate father but Estella's real father. This arrangement is again reminiscent of that which binds father Quilp, the Marchioness, and Dick Swiveller together. In *Great Expectations,* in other words, the prospective fathers-in-law are stacked up two deep, like airplanes in a holding pattern. Pip and Herbert Pocket each have a prospective father-in-law upstairs, with Pip's the topmost. This is appropriate since he is the book's central figure, after all, and Magwitch is not only the father of the girl Pip wants and can't have but he's also acting as Pip's father by providing for him his expectations.

To turn back to *Martin Chuzzlewit,* it is even worth noting that when Pecksniff makes his speech about phallic wooden legs we see him from *below.* He has been dallying with Mrs. Todgers among her lodgers, and has gotten drunk, and has been carried upstairs and put to bed. But he is in the happy rather than the somnolent stage of drunkenness and before he goes to sleep he wanders out again onto the stairway landing in his nightdress to make the following oration to the assembled lodgers and to Mrs. Todgers down below.

"This is very soothing," said Mr. Pecksniff, after a pause. "Extremely so. Cool and refreshing; particularly to the legs! The legs of the human subject, my friends, are a beautiful production. Compare them with wooden legs, and observe the difference between the anatomy of nature and the anatomy of art. Do you know," said Mr. Pecksniff, leaning over the banisters, with an odd recollection of his familiar manner among new pupils at home, "that I should very much like to see Mrs. Todgers' notion of a wooden leg, if perfectly agreeable to herself!"

It is a veiled, comic, displaced but emphatic indecent proposal. This is even more true when one remembers that this is, after all, a Victorian novel, and that was an era when legs were so charged with suppressed sexuality they had to be kept fully covered, even on pianos, and could be referred to only as *limbs*. The wooden leg is symbolic at once of the father's great phallus and of the castration of the father, and, under certain circumstances, of the son also. Mr. Pecksniff, Silas Wegg, and old Gruff and Glum represent various aspects of the father, and so do Mr. Barley and Mr. Barkis and Mr. Bray. By this time it is surely clear that in choosing the names Barley and Barkis and Bray, Dickens is anagrammatically underlining in a characteristic way the fact that in all three cases he is thinking of essentially the same part of the father. But we have as yet said little about the cutting down of the Beanstalk, the mythical castration which makes the wooden leg necessary.

To introduce this side of the symbolic meaning of wooden legs, it is useful to turn to another pretty girl and her father, Dolly (and the name connotes a function as well as a personality) Varden and Gabriel Varden of *Barnaby Rudge*. Just as the mother appears symbolically incarnated in two forms, as the negative, denying, repulsive loathly old hag, and as the positive, affirming, attractive young girl, so also there are two versions of the father. The negative, denying father keeps the girl mother away from the boy. Bray, Barkis and Barley are of this type. Murdstone provides perhaps their most emphatic representative. The positive, affirming, giving, loving father appears on the other hand in Wilkins Micawber, in Mr. Pickwick, in Noddy Boffin, the Golden Dustman in *Our Mutual Friend,* and in Gabriel Varden. In addition to being a novel about the Gordon Riots, mental retardation, and conflict between fathers and sons, *Barnaby Rudge* is a novel about ways in which women castrate their men.

Gabriel Varden and his wife, Martha, are the central embodiments of this theme, and from them it transfers itself outward. First it is transferred to their daughter, Dolly, who is, in the Loathly Hag scheme, not altogether distinct from Mrs. Varden's youthful self, and then it is transferred to Mr. Varden's apprentice, to Mrs. Varden's maid, and to various other people. At the opening of the novel, we discover that Mrs. Varden "was a lady of what is commonly called an uncertain temper." She makes her husband miserable. Even the neighbors all more or less observe of Mrs. Varden

> that a tumble down some half-dozen rounds in the world's ladder—such as the breaking of the bank in which her husband kept his money, or some little fall of that kind— would be the making of her, and could hardly fail to render her one of the most agreeable companions in existence.

This is a pretty fair description of what does indeed happen to Martha Varden to improve her relations with her husband, Gabriel, and with the rest of the world. Humility, submission, obedience are, among other things, an erotic necessity. The very language of the description refers to the nature of the remedy that is needed. It does so partly through the symbolic imagery of props, and partly through the kind of verbal play which occurs both in dreams and in wit. As we have already seen, this sort of thing constitutes one of the distinctive characteristics of Dickens' genius.

Women's unconsciously motivated falling in everyday life, or their dreams of falling, express unconscious desire to surrender to erotic temptation. In dreams, stairs, steps, ladders, and even piano keyboards for which the keys are like steps, and motion up or down them refer either to copulation or to orgasm. In the fourth chapter we shall discuss further the sexual significance of money and the places it is kept, but we have already seen enough of this sort of thing to perceive that the "breaking of the bank in which her husband kept his money" would, indeed, "be the making of her." What Mrs. Varden needs to do so very badly is to submit to Gabriel in bed. Gabriel Varden is a master locksmith, and in dreams keys often symbolize the male genital organ, while locks just as often refer to the female organ.

This seems to me to be a good place for a digressive reminder of the multiplicity of meanings and levels of meanings simultaneously invested in the novels and their props. The sexual meaning is only one of these. It is not necessarily always the most important one. It is, however, one which may easily be missed. There is always a literal level of meaning. The fact that meaning from the level of unconscious fantasy may be invested some of the time in some of the props does not for a moment deprive those same props of their specific, concrete, literal meaning and dramatic function in Dickens' fiction. Gabriel Varden's role as a locksmith is of literal as well as symbolic importance in the novel.

Mr. Varden lives in a house with his locksmith's shop downstairs in the basement. Early in the novel we see him

> gazing disconsolately at a great wooden emblem of a key, painted in a vivid yellow to resemble gold, which dangled from the house-front, and swung to and fro with a mournful creaking noise, as if complaining that it had nothing to unlock.

In the fourth chapter we shall go further into the sexual significance of gold, but in any event Gabriel's thoughts could not possibly be more transparent here. In dreams the dreamer commonly sees his body as a house, with his various organs often appearing to be parts of the house. Martha has just been scolding Gabriel for much of the night and has certainly given him no opportunity to unlock her lock with his formidable golden key.

That this is a fairly chronic state of affairs in their relationship is evident. It is especially frustrating to Gabriel because on his way home the night before his sexual desires and anticipations had been up, and revealed themselves in the dream he dreamt as he drove his horse and cart.

> He had roused himself once, when the horse stopped until the turnpike gate was opened, and had cried a lusty "good night" to the toll-keeper; but then he woke out of a dream about picking a lock in the stomach of the Great Mogul, and even when he did wake, mixed up the turnpike man with his mother-in-law who had been dead twenty years.

He has been confusing thoughts of a girl and her mother, and reflections about various kinds of people who let you go through the gate. He has obviously been thinking about his wife, who has acquired for him some of the dominating qualities of "the Great Mogul," in terms of the earlier, better days when they first courted and married and he took her from her mother's house. At that time she more nearly resembled what her daughter Dolly looks like now.

For a long time through the earlier half of the novel Martha lords it unmercifully over her husband. The outward and visible sign of her castrating powers is her box made to resemble a little red-brick dwelling house with a yellow roof. It is used to hold money for the Protestant Association which Lord Gordon heads. Its roof is yellow like gold, please note, and it is a money-box, like Gabriel's bank. It is only when the Protestant Association so manifestly brings the riots about that Gabriel's manhood reasserts itself.

Martha, realizing her own fault, with deep feelings of guilt withdraws her own, long, improperly asserted dominance. She tries to hide its emblem, the flagrant money box, under her chair, and "hid the same still further, with the skirts of her dress." (Where it should have been kept all along.) But Gabriel owes it to himself and to his family, and, indeed, to his whole topsy-turvy rioting world of civil insurrection, to reassert the rightful dominance of manhood, and so he makes her give him the box and he destroys it.

> So he dropped the red-brick dwellinghouse on the floor, and setting his heel upon it, crushed it into pieces.

Thereafter matters slowly turn for the better in the course of the novel, and at the end, when all is *right* again, or as right as it can be, we see Gabriel's legs for the first time. He has "slept off his fatigue" and (perhaps like Mr. Barkis) had "a nap" and "a quiet chat with Mrs. Varden on everything that had happened, was happening, or about to happen, within the sphere of their domestic concern." He has become "the rosiest, cosiest, merriest, heartiest, best-contented old buck, in Great Britain or out of it."

> There he sat, with his beaming eye on Mrs. V., and his shining face suffused with gladness, and his capacious waistcoat smiling in every wrinkle, and his jovial humour peeping from under the table in the very plumpness of his legs: a sight to turn the vinegar of misanthropy into purest milk of human kindness.

That is to say, comically, symbolically, and with the most wonderful displacement, a massive ejaculation. But he is the lucky one in the novel. Virtually every other male is castrated one way or another.

Simon Tappertit has provided himself secretly with a big key to his master's front door so he can come and go clandestinely. Mrs. Varden's maid Miggs fills the lock with coal-dust so Sim, returning early in the morning, cannot get his key into the lock. Early in the novel Miggs wishes that she could persuade 10,000 maidens to join her in committing suicide so the men would be deprived of them. It is Miggs who is acquainted with a dustman who has lost both hands and has two hooks instead (it is not legs alone—and their loss—that are important). It is Miggs who disables Mr. Varden's gun with table beer so it won't fire. It is Miggs who finally achieves the height of her sexually destructive desires by becoming a woman jailor, locking away any number of women from the access of the men, and, furthermore, sadistically torturing the pretty, desirable ones.

Most of the symbolic castrations in the novel have to do with Dolly Varden, her mother Martha's alter ego. Insofar as *Barnaby Rudge* expresses by analogy the circumstances of the Loathly Hag, Dolly is the young and luscious woman, her mother the old hag. Every male who desires Dolly is punished for it. Maypole Hugh, Chester's bastard son, is sexually the most energetic male in the novel. He is curiously identified with the Maypole itself, the most outstanding phallus in the novel, the nearest to a Beanstalk, and consequently one which, in a book about conflict between fathers and sons and about women castrating their men, is inevitably cut down.

We actually do get to see Hugh climb the Maypole in a manner significantly like Jack climbing the Beanstalk. Hugh is in some ways the most rebellious of all the sons, the one most out to steal the father's good. He takes on all society. Old John Willet wishes to show off Hugh to Mr. Chester. He commands him:

> "You, sir! Bring that horse here, and go and hang my wig on the weathercock, to show this gentleman whether you're one of the lively sort or not."
>
> Hugh made no answer, but throwing the bridle to his master, and snatching his wig from his head, in a manner so unceremonious and hasty that the action discomposed Mr. Willet not a little, though performed at his own special desire, climbed nimbly to the very summit of the maypole before the house, and hanging the wig upon the weathercock, sent it twirling round like a roasting-jack. Having achieved this performance, he cast it on the ground, and sliding down the pole with inconceivable rapidity, alighted on his feet almost as soon as it had touched the earth.

When Bella Wilfer marries John Rokesmith in *Our Mutual Friend*, we shall see that the wedding dinner is served by a headwaiter who is

a solemn gentleman in black clothes and a white cravat, who looked much more like a clergyman than *the* clergyman, and seemed to have mounted a great deal higher in the church: not to say, scaled the steeple.

It is Jack climbing up the Beanstalk to rival and to threaten the father, and that headwaiter, like Hugh, represents Jack. Hair in dreams, or fur in dreams, often refers to pubic hair. Hats generally refer to women's genitals, more rarely to men's. It is with pubic hair that Hugh decorates the maypole. Even though it is from a man's head that he take the wig, it is an emphatically vulvic wig Hugh twirls atop the object Dickens ostentatiously does not describe as a weather*vane,* but as a weather*cock.* Hugh has a frightful hankering for Dolly, molests her at one point, and helps to abduct her at another. The form of castration he is made to suffer is hanging.

It is Joe Willet who finally wins Dolly and weds her, and even Joe loses an arm. But the one who desires Dolly the most is Simon Tappertit, and he is punished the most.

We have already seen him provide himself with a secret key to the lock of the front door of his master's house. That is, in dream language, he seeks access to those female genitals which belong properly only to Gabriel Varden. In dream terms they are the same, or at any rate virtually indistinguishable. They represent both parts of the Loathly Hag, both Dolly and Martha. It is Simon Tappertit who gets the rioters to try to persuade Varden to pick the great lock in the main gate of Newgate prison. He does this because he knows Gabriel helped design and build that lock. In other words, that lock, like the lock to Gabriel's front door, belongs peculiarly to Gabriel. An assault upon it is another version of the same sexual assault upon the locks which belong to Gabriel. Varden says that if he should stoop to picking the Newgate lock at the command of the rioters his hands would drop off at the wrists and Sim should wear them on his shoulders for epaulettes. This creates an image of the two hands, cut off (like Miggs' friend the dustman), one on either of Sim's shoulders, with his head rising between them. Symbolically this implies that Varden is saying to Sim that before he can get into *that* lock Sim will have to wear his master's testicles. And we shall have further occasion to see that the symbolic investiture of the son with his father's genitals is an act of the greatest moment, for it must occur just before he gets the girl who is just like the girl that married dear old dad.

Poor, vain, mean Simon Tappertit is in love with his legs and thinks they are irresistible to women. Blind Stagg (and we all remember Oedipus and the relationship of eyes to testicles and blinding to castration whether in dreams or in folk-lore) makes a prediction about Simon's legs when he drops on one knee and gently smooths the calves of Sim's legs:

When I touch my own afterwards . . . I hate 'em . . . they've no more shape than wooden legs, besides these models of my noble captain's.

Stagg is not only symbolically castrated in his blindness, but in his legs' resemblance to wooden legs as well. However, his predictive comparison of Sim's legs to wooden ones is reiterated when Sim wanders among the skittles and his followers hold "his little shins in dumb respect" and he "muses among the ninepins," the wooden ninepins. Sim is as active as Hugh in the abduction of Dolly Varden. His punishment is to lose both of his legs, to get two wooden ones, and to become a bootblack besides.

Simon thus has two wooden legs, like old Gruff and Glum, or like Silas Wegg if his ligneosity waxes. In dreams the reiteration of images of sticks generally betokens an emphasis upon both meanings attached to the wooden phallus. The multiplication constitutes a magical attempt to ward off the threat of castration, and the attempt to ward it off indicates an emphatic expression of how inevitable the castration is, how well deserved, and how soon it will occur. One wants to look, therefore, especially closely at the multiple amputees in the novels, or, for that matter, at any other occurrences of reduplicated prosthetic devices.

There is, for example, only one church in Coketown in *Hard Times* that displays any individuality, and that is "the New Church; a stuccoed edifice with a square steeple over the door, terminating in four short pinnacles like florid wooden legs." And when Josiah Bounderby and Louisa Gradgrind perpetrate their loveless union, the ceremony is performed "in the church of the florid wooden legs." Bounderby's four florid wooden legs are allied to Swiveller's hundred thousand games of cribbage. This display of four wooden phalluses at once expresses Josiah Bounderby's sexual excitement at getting so young a girl into his bed and also his punishment for the guilty act of marrying a girl young enough to be his daughter. It furthermore associates the Bounderby-Gradgrind nuptials with the Wilfer-Rokesmith and Dombey-Gay ones with respect to the presence of wooden legs. And we shall shortly see that there is a wooden leg present at Florence Dombey's father's wedding to Edith Skewton Granger.

It will, indeed, become more and more clear that a

Florence Dombey and Susan Nipper Being Ogled Shamelessly by the Little Wooden Midshipman

number of these weddings in the later novels all come together as a single event which occupies a position of some
prominence in the sexual map which underlies all of
Dickens' novels. For the present we may note that in addition to the wooden-legged man at Florence's wedding,
who is a dim anticipation of old Gruff and Glum at Bella's,
there is another wooden-legged man in Florence's experience. In *Dombey and Son,* Florence and Susan Nipper
visited Uncle Sol Gills and Walter Gay just before the sail-
ing of the Son and Heir. Uncle Sol attended her "lovingly
to the legs of the Wooden Midshipman, and there resigned
her to Walter, who was ready to escort her and Susan
Nipper to the coach." The statue which is the signpost for
Uncle Sol's shop, the Little Wooden Midshipman, and
Walter Gay are of course one and the same person. The
Midshipman's wooden legs represent Walter's phallus,
frustrated for the time being.

There is a coming together of the wooden leg and
cherub images which further associates Dombey's wedding
to Edith with Bella's to John Rokesmith. Reginald Wilfer,
Bella's father, is extensively referred to as "cherubic." The
cherubic aspect of his being comes very much to the fore
at his daughter's wedding.

For Gruff and Glum, though most events acted on him
simply as tobacco-stoppers, pressing down and condensing
the quids within him, might be imagined to trace a family
resemblance between the cherubs in the church architecture, and the cherub in the white waistcoat. Some
resemblance of old valentines, wherein a cherub, less appropriately attired for a proverbially uncertain climate,
had been seen conducting lovers to the altar, might have
been fancied to inflame the ardour of his timber toes.
Be it as it might, he gave his moorings the slip, and followed in chase.

The cherub went before, all beaming smiles; Bella and John Rokesmith followed; Gruff and Glum stuck to them like wax. For years the wings of his mind had gone to look after the legs of his body; but Bella had brought them back for him per steamer, and they were spread again.

He was a slow sailor on a wind of happiness, but he took a cross cut for the rendezvous, and pegged away as if he were scoring furiously at cribbage.

The cherub helps promote the cribbage game. He is a childlike figure, and as we shall see, such figures in dreams sometimes symbolize the genitals. A cherub in the church architecture is likely to have a wooden leg much like the Little Wooden Midshipman's. Indeed, Miss Tox sneaks in surreptitiously to watch Dombey utterly destroy her own hopes by marrying Edith, and as Dombey "looks up at the organ, Miss Tox in the gallery shrinks behind the fat legs of a cherub on a monument, with cheeks like a young Wind." The juxtaposition of the parts is not quite right, but the parts mentioned as Dombey looks at the "organ" are a fat upright member and two puffed out rounded surfaces right next to each other. It appears, in fact, to be a symbolic penis and testicles from behind which Miss Tox has chosen forlornly to witness Dombey's union with Edith. There is the additional element that these nuptial events are likely to be observed by clandestine watchers.

We recall Dick Swiveller's drunken fantasy in which he saw his symbolic father, Daniel Quilp, as a kind of vision of the progenitive organs. Here at Bella's wedding her father appears in a similarly symbolic and visionary way. Throughout the chapter in *Our Mutual Friend* in which Bella's wedding is described, she is seen repeatedly playing coquettishly with her cherubic father. She is, as it were, playing with her father's genitals. This accounts for a large part of the highly charged visionary and ecstatic quality of the chapter.

As we have observed, in dreams children often represent the genitals, and beating a child, or playing with a child, in dreams quite often represents masturbation or some other such form of manipulation of the genitals. Reginald Wilfer is almost always referred to either in terms of his being a child or in terms of his being a cherub.

> If the conventional Cherub could ever grow up and be clothed, he might be photographed as a portrait of Wilfer. His chubby, smooth, innocent appearance was a reason for his always being treated with condescension when he was not put down. A stranger entering his own poor house at about ten o'clock P.M. might have been surprised to find him sitting up to supper. So boyish was he in his curves and proportions, that his old schoolmaster meeting him in Cheapside, might have been unable to withstand the temptation of caning him on the spot.

He is not only a set of male genitals, but he is such a set as it is almost impossible to resist masturbating.

His daughter, Bella, obviously cannot resist playing with him. The sexual play with the cherub father creates sexual excitement in part expressed by displacement to the other father-like figure, old Gruff and Glum. Flying in dreams sometimes signifies erections. When old Gruff and Glum finds the sight of Bella bringing back to him the wings of his mind, from such close proximity to his legs, and spread so widely, it is clear that Bella has performed the miracle of giving a castrated man, indeed, father, an erection. It is a fitting climax in a novel which largely deals, as we shall see, with resurrection. It is no wonder the chapter is so intense, so ecstatic, so visionary. As was the case with the many hundred thousand games of cribbage played by Dick Swiveller and the Marchioness, so it is also here. There is a wish so strong it has to be fulfilled. The major difference between the two is that here in the later novel the fulfillment of the wish does not take so cryptic a form. It is more out in the open, as we would expect it to be in a later dream in a series of dreams.

CHAPTER III

THE BOILING LIQUID

Sexual Fire

THE PRECEDING CHAPTER has enabled us to see a little way into the unconscious ideation at work behind the ecstatic description of Bella Wilfer's wedding to John Rokesmith in *Our Mutual Friend*. We have developed some, but not all, of the necessary connotations held by wooden legs and other phallic symbols. This book is not designed to be exhaustive, either with respect to the props or with respect to their hidden sexual meanings. There are a great many of both which we will not mention at all here, or will touch only lightly.

The book demonstrates the fact that some of the props some of the time serve as a kind of hieroglyphic language which reveals a sexual mythology that is an important part of the meaning which shapes and inspires Dickens' fiction. This happens in a way that can only be glimpsed dimly, if it is indeed seen at all, without the translation of that language. This book is meant to elucidate the essential themes of this underlying sexual mythology although it in no way exhausts the topic.

The focus of the discussion throughout this and the following chapter is *Our Mutual Friend* and, especially, the fourth chapter of its fourth part in which Bella Wilfer and John Rokesmith are married. This is the target at which the discussion always aims. The actual progress of that discussion, however, will sometimes be found to proceed along indirect and circuitous routes. The associative trains of thought which link the props together are not infrequently devious. We have already seen that in order to understand the significance of old Gruff and Glum scoring furiously at cribbage, we had to investigate the displacement of psychic intensities in the *Old Curiosity Shop,* a novel distant in time and apparently quite different in theme.

We have discovered that the process of analysis consists in following the trails of the props through the novels, and in finding the hidden identities of the characters with whom the props are most prominently associated. We have partially identified Silas Wegg and his surrogate, old Gruff and Glum, and we understand some of the significance of their wooden legs. In order to enlarge that understanding further we shall need to investigate the identities of two other characters in the novel, Mr. Venus and Jenny Wren. In them certain of Bella Wilfer's magical qualities appear to be duplicated, and some aspects of her hidden identity appear to be displaced. In order to do this we must again turn to other novels, to *Martin Chuzzlewit,* to the *Old Curiosity Shop,* and to *Barnaby Rudge.*

Barnaby Rudge is, as we have seen, a novel about struggle between fathers and sons, and between wives and husbands, and the relations these struggles have to civil insurrection. It is also a novel full of violence, and, in its concluding chapters, of mob violence which appears to be climaxed by a destructive fire of extraordinary dramatic nature.

There are obviously a variety of levels of meaning involved. For one thing, the fires did in fact occur historically, and their literal significance is not their least important one. It is true here, as indeed everywhere else throughout this book, that my interpretation of Dickens' props does not imply that this is the only or even necessarily the most important meaning contained in the material. It is simply *one* level of meaning that is often not easy to perceive. When perceived, however, it does contribute to a better understanding of Dickens' art.

There are three particularly intense scenes of destruction by fire in *Barnaby Rudge*: the destruction of the Warren, the burning of Newgate, and the burning of the purple-faced vintner's wine and liquor. Our discussion of Warren's Blacking and of Varden's locks has suggested some of the probable significance contained within the first two. In addition to the generalized dream relationship between fire and heat and the idea of the erotic, the smashing of the vintner's casks and the burning of his liquor are described with special intensity.

The gutters of the street and every crack and fissure in the stones, ran with scorching spirit, which being dammed up by busy hands, overflowed the road and pavement, and formed a great pool, in which the people dropped down dead by dozens. They lay in heaps all round this fearful pond, husbands and wives, fathers and sons, mothers and daughters, women with children in their arms and babies at their breasts, and drank until they died. While some stooped with their lips to the brink and never raised their

The Burning Liquor

heads again, others sprang up from their fiery draught, and danced, half in a mad triumph, and half in the agony of suffocation, until they fell and steeped their corpses in the liquor that had killed them. Nor was even this the worst or most appalling kind of death that happened on this fatal night. From the burning cellars, where they drank out of hats, pails, buckets, tubs, and shoes, some men were drawn, alive, but all alight from head to foot; who, in their unendurable anguish and suffering, making for anything that had the look of water, rolled, hissing, in this hideous lake, and splashed up liquid fire which lapped in all it met with as it ran along the surface, and neither spared the living nor the dead.

Just before the vintner's house is stormed, he and Mr. Haredale look down from the roof-top of the house into the hellish sea of rioters threatening their very lives as well as the house. Hugh is in the center of the mob, and is one of its chief leaders. The vintner indicates that there is a secret way out through which they can escape:

Through the cellars, there's a kind of passage into the back street by which we roll casks in and out.

They descend to these lower regions and encounter Edward Chester and Joe Willet there. They escape with them from the rioters who are now beginning to break into the cellars.

So when they had crawled through the passage indicated by the vintner (which was a mere shelving-trap for the admission of casks) and had managed with some difficulty to unchain and raise the door at the upper end, they emerged into the street without being observed or interrupted.

It is an escape through a birth-canal, a rebirth, in fact.

To understand why this should be so, and the significance it has in the novel, we need to remember that this
is the first reappearance of Edward Chester and Joe Willet
after an absence of several years and hundreds of pages.
They have returned just in time for the riots. They have
been pretending to be rioters, and from that undercover
position have several times in several ways been able to
foil the rioters' aims. In particular, Edward Chester has
just been able to strike down Hugh from his horse, thus
saving the life of the good father, Gabriel Varden, and,
indirectly, aiding the cause of the escape of the vintner
and of Mr. Haredale.

This last is important, because one of the secondary
themes of the plot is the tension—it is not too much to
call it a feud—between the Haredale and Chester families.
This has led the elder Chester to forbid his son, and
Mr. Haredale to forbid his niece, to think about each other.
Edward and Emma are, heaven help them, star crossed
lovers. This feud is also related to the civil insurrection
and the prejudice against Roman Catholics. Both are
motivating factors that led Edward's father, Sir John
Chester, to inspire Hugh to lead the rioters in the burning
of Haredale's Warren. In addition to being a personal
enemy to Chester, Haredale is a Roman Catholic. Just before their escape through the passageway, young Ned
Chester has taken the first crucial step toward a reconciliation with Mr. Haredale. The ultimate possibility of
his marrying Emma Haredale is thus reborn.

Joe Willet has also accomplished the beginning of a sort
of reconcilation with *his* father, through the purple-faced
vintner who is a kind of surrogate for old John Willet. It
is these reconcilations of some of the novel's critical father

and son conflicts which brings about the rebirth symbolized by the escape through the birth-canal, that is, through the passageway ordinarily used only by the casks. Even the difficulty they encounter in getting out at the upper end helps to indicate that this is a birth trauma, a rebirth for them out of hell into a new life.

If the passageway is a vagina, then the firm, well-made, solid casks of good strong beer or wine or spirits which normally have admission there are phallic. They are wooden like wooden legs, but they are even better as images of the phallus because they are full of intoxicating, life-giving liquid that is fiery and exciting. Furthermore, when they are filled with wine, their contents resembles blood. This association is clearly established in *A Tale of Two Cities* when a large cask of wine is smashed outside the Defarge wine shop.

In *Martin Chuzzlewit,* John Westlock's courting of adorable little Ruth Pinch, to whose sexual significance we shall return, reaches the point of physical contact, and trembles on the verge of a proposal of marriage. At this point the excuse for his picking her up in his arms is provided in this manner:

> There were two good-tempered burly draymen letting down big butts of beer into a cellar somewhere; and when John helped her—almost lifted her—the lightest, easiest, neatest thing you ever saw—across the rope, they said he owed them a good turn for giving him the chance. Celestial draymen!

The draymen are celestial, in large part, because those big butts of beer going through the aperature down below are representative of sexual intercourse.

Again it is in *Barnaby Rudge* that we can see that even Simon Tappertit's sexual aspirations and frustrations are reflected by means of this symbol.

> As certain liquors, confined in casks too cramped in their dimensions, will ferment, and fret, and chafe in their imprisonment, so the spiritual essence or soul of Mr. Tappertit would sometimes fume within that precious cask, his body, until, with great foam and froth and splutter, it would force a vent, and carry all before it.

Dickens is primarily describing Sim's overweening ambition, but the image resembles that of an ejaculation. In view of the absence of any external agent of friction, or even excitation, it seems likely that the ejaculation is the result of masturbation or of a nocturnal emission. Later on in *Barnaby Rudge,* after the Maypole Inn has been castrated of its maypole, its condition is further expressed when old John Willet dimly perceives that

> even the stout Dutch kegs, overthrown and lying empty in dark corners, seemed the mere husks of good fellows whose jollity had departed, and who could kindle with a friendly glow no more.

But the prop behaves consistently elsewhere in the novels, too.

In *David Copperfield,* at the time Murdstone's courting of David's mother, Clara, first looms upon David's consciousness, he sees "Peggotty, standing as stiff as a barrel in the centre of the room, with a candlestick in her hand." In *Little Dorrit,* the loveless house to which Arthur Clennam returns contains a number of "empty beer-casks hoary with cobwebs, and empty wine-bottles with fur and fungus choking up their throats."

The prop figures very largely in *Great Expectations,* especially in connection with Miss Havisham and Estella, who are practising a particularly sophisticated and flagrant form of emasculation. As one would expect in a later novel, it is much more out in the open. The opening scene of the novel contains two black things on its bleak horizon. They "seemed to be standing upright" and one was "the beacon by which the sailors steered—like an unhooped cask up on a pole—an ugly thing when you were near it." It is suggestive of the beacon by which Pip steers his course of frustration and unrequited love toward his star, Estella.

> . . . she seemed to be everywhere. For, when I yielded to the temptation presented by the casks, and began to walk on them, I saw *her* walking on them at the end of the yard of casks.

It is Miss Havisham's Satis House which is so well stocked with empty, disused, wasted casks upon which Estella has been reared to walk so insolently. Later it is by "the wilderness of casks . . . miniature swamps and pools of water upon those that stood on end, I made my way to the ruined garden." Finally, at the auction after Miss Havisham's death, Pip sees the auctioneer's clerk walking on the casks counting them.

Pip's friend Wemmick, who helps him accomplish the one successful and unmitigated bit of good that comes out of his "expectations" (getting Herbert Pocket set up in business), is a wooden man. There is some redeeming good in him, for he was not, after all, "brought up to the

Law, but to the Wine-Coopering." It is Wemmick's original potential ability to put casks together so they will be tight and stout and new and not leak their precious contents that serves to redeem the bleak prospect of the sailor's beacon, the unhooped cask.

It is out of these casks, furthermore, that the burning liquids come. It is possible to follow the train of associations started by these in a direction which will lead toward the identification of Mr. Venus and of Jenny Wren. The scenes of the burning of the vintner's house in *Barnaby Rudge* are matched, in the same novel, by the scenes of the burners of Haredale's Warren. They paddle in the flames, drunkenly, as though they were in water. Their heads are melted like wax as the molten lead pours from the roof. They are matched in a much later novel, *A Tale of Two Cities,* by the boiling of the molten lead and iron in the marble basin of the St. Evremonde fountain. But the most striking feature of the burning, fiery liquor at the destruction of the vintner's house is that it is drunk up by the rioting people in a kind of suicidal frenzy.

The drinking of boiling or fiery liquid is a very curious phenomenon which appears rarely in Dickens' novels, but, when it does, it has deep significance. At the very least is the associative implication that the same kind of people do it from one novel to another. The hidden, inner identity is the same, however much other outer qualities may differ. In the pursuit of this significance we shall have occasion to observe still another way in which dreams and certain qualities in Dickens' novels behave similarly.

Ever since Edmund Wilson drew attention to them the importance of the interpolated tales in *Pickwick* and in the other novels has been frequently noted. These are usually tales of great passion, often dark and violent. Sometimes they express thematic material which underlies the action of the host novel in which they appear, or which makes illuminating comment upon that action. In *Nicholas Nickleby,* for instance, Baron Grogzwig's interview with the demon of despair and suicide is an interpolated tale which anticipates the way uncle Ralph Nickleby so passionately destroys himself. Miss Wade's personal confession constitutes an interpolated tale in *Little Dorrit.* It makes a significant comment upon the deep passions working inside Arthur Clennam and his stepmother. Alexandre Manette's damning indictment of the St. Evremonde family in the document Defarge took from his former cell in the Bastille is a working device of the plot. It is also an interpolated tale which makes explicit the injury done Lucie's father by Charles Darnay's family, a statement, in other words, of the father-son conflict.

Sometimes the interpolated tales embody themes to which later novels will return again and again. Sometimes they employ minute details associated with a single kind of situation which occurs over and over again. In the Tale of the Queer Client told by old Jack Bamber to Mr. Pickwick, George Heyling's wife takes her child to the nearby old bridge to try to amuse him with the river scenery, but mostly weeps over their hopeless predicament. Many other debtor's dependents throughout the novels seek consolation on bridges. When the Micawbers are in prison for debt little David Copperfield and the Orfling lounge together and try to comfort each other on old London Bridge. It is on the Iron Bridge that Arthur Clennam seeks to console Little Dorrit about her father's apparently hopeless imprisonment for debt in the Marshalsea. It is there that she really falls in love with him.

Whichever kind they may be, these interpolated tales resemble dreams within dreams. They generally deal with material to which one part of the psyche is especially desirous of denying reality. The reality, consequently, is most emphatically, though negatively, affirmed. This mechanism works on the rule that the stronger the inhibition the stronger the impulse or idea being inhibited. The one which concerns us here is the first occurrence in the novels of the drinking of fiery liquid. It takes place during Gabriel Grub's Rip Van Winkleish nightmare in one of *Pickwick*'s interpolated tales.

> "Cold to-night," said the king of goblins, "very cold. A glass of something warm, here!"
>
> At this command, half a dozen officious goblins, with a perpetual smile upon their faces, whom Gabriel Grub imagined to be courtiers, on that account, hastily disappeared, and presently returned with a goblet of liquid fire, which they presented to the king.
>
> "Ah!" cried the goblin, whose cheeks and throat were transparent, as he tossed down the flame, "This warms one, indeed! Bring a bumper of the same, for Mr. Grub."
>
> It was in vain for the unfortunate sexton to protest that he was not in the habit of taking anything warm at night; one of the goblins held him while another poured the blazing liquid down his throat; the whole assembly screeched with laughter as he coughed and choked, and wiped away the tears which gushed plentifully from his eyes, after swallowing the burning draught.

The next occurrence of this sort of thing is in *Oliver Twist*, when Monks, who exhibits all of the earmarks of a creature out of hell, makes Bumble drink a steaming hot jorum that brings the water to his eyes.

It is in the *Old Curiosity Shop*, however, that Daniel Quilp is a much more emphatic reincarnation of the goblin king. He drinks boiling tea without winking. Later he urges the fiery Schiedam liquor on Dick Swiveller:

"Is it good?" said Quilp . . . "is it strong and fiery? Does it make you wink, and choke, and your eyes water, and your breath come short—does it?"

Much later on Sampson Brass tremulously finds Daniel Quilp in his counting house heating some rum in a little sauce pan, and watching it to prevent its boiling over.

. . . Mr. Quilp raised the hot saucepan to his lips, and deliberately drank off all the spirit it contained, which might have been in quantity about half a pint, and had been but a moment before, when he took it off the fire, bubbling and hissing fiercely.

Quilp then forces Brass to sip some, making his face turn red, tears flow, and making him cough terribly. He makes him drink still more to honor "the lovely Sarah," and Brass passes out. Sampson Brass' role with Daniel Quilp here, as elsewhere, is analogous to Grub's role with the goblin. And still later Quilp drinks another draught of boiling punch "as if it were fair water and cooling to his parched mouth," and then he goes out and drowns.

Dreams have a way of employing vivid images for a person or function or relationship which express exactly the quality which is pertinent to the meaning of the dream thought. In the fictional characterization of dreams, the author, that is, the unconscious mind, employs the technique of caricature, or at least a kind of symbolic emphasis quite like caricature, much as Dickens does. It is not surprising to find the qualities of the goblin king recreated in Monks and Daniel Quilp. But it is curious to find them quite specifically and exactly recreated in Jenny Wren. We shall come to see that her embodiment of these Quilpish and goblinesque qualities is of the greatest importance in understanding her nature, her identity, and her roles.

At one point Jenny observes to Lizzie Hexam that if she were to discover that her knight-errant lover should turn out to be an alcoholic like her father and grandfather:

> . . . I'd make a spoon red hot, and I'd have some boiling liquor bubbling in a saucepan, and I'd take it out hissing, and I'd open his mouth with the other hand—or perhaps he'd sleep with his mouth ready open—and I'd pour it down his throat, and blister it and choke him.

And this is part and parcel of her earlier threats to pepper the children who taunt her, and of her later actual peppering of Fledgeby. There is inside Jenny Wren, in other words, an adumbration of the same identity that pursued the pure child, Little Nell, with the intent of ravaging her purity.

It is not surprising to find that although he does not appear to drink such liquids, Bradley Headstone, in the psychic content of frustrated Miss Peecher's day-dream filled geography lessons,

> would come triumphantly flying out of Vesuvius and Aetna ahead of the lava, and would boil unharmed in the hot springs of Iceland, and would float majestically down the Ganges and the Nile.

The critical words here are "boiled unharmed," for if there is any distinction being made by the association of these images, it is that certain rare, demonic beings like the goblin and Quilp and Headstone are capable of dealing directly with raw, flaming, untamed, unrepressed, unashamed passionate sexual force without burning themselves, whereas ordinary mortals exposed to such elemental forces "dropped down dead by dozens."

It is furthermore the case that the handlers of the stuff, the goblin, Quilp, and Jenny Wren, sadistically enjoy inflicting it upon others. It is not surprising to find these qualities expressed in a muted, but unmistakable way, in the man whose name is the name of the goddess of love. In *Our Mutual Friend*, Silas Wegg repeatedly finds Mr. Venus drinking boiling hot tea, and although it makes his eyes water, it doesn't seem to hurt him. But Mr. Venus also uses the same boiling liquids in another way, and that is in the practice of his art to boil the meat off the bones he so beautifully articulates. This is a thought which rather frightens Silas, as well it might, especially in view of Venus' intimate professional acquaintance with Wegg's leg. Mr. Venus, in other words, is like Jenny and the goblin and Quilp in that he can handle the stuff unharmed, and that he can also in the course of his professional activities not only inflict it on others, but employ it to dismember them. As was the case with Jenny Wren, this mild mannered little man has in him something of the same identity that so strongly desired to rape Little Nell.

There is another train of associations parallel to this one and joining together many of the same characters as well as some other, related ones. It will shed further light on the identity of Mr. Venus whose nature will prove to be of importance in our fuller understanding of *Our Mutual Friend*. This line of associated images consists of the roasting, toasting, broiling which relate to cooking fire in much the same way that boiling liquids do. Fagin is emphatically associated with such imagery in *Oliver Twist*. When Oliver first sees him, it is as the center of the following scene:

The walls and ceiling of the room were perfectly black with age and dirt. There was a deal table before the fire. . . . In a frying-pan, which was on the fire, and which was secured to the mantelshelf by a string, some sausages were cooking; and standing over them, with a toasting-fork in his hand, was a very old shrivelled Jew, whose villainous-looking and repulsive face was obscured by a quantity of matted red hair. He was dressed in a greasy flannel gown, with his throat bare . . . round the table were four or five boys . . . [who] turned round and grinned at Oliver. So did the Jew himself, toasting-fork in hand.

It is the traditional kind of greeting Satan accords visitors to hell. Fagin is often seen cooking. The very next morning:

There was no other person in the room but the old Jew, who was boiling some coffee in a saucepan for breakfast, and whistling softly to himself as he stirred it round and round, with an iron spoon.

Again, later, Oliver sees "the old man, who was stooping over the fire toasting a piece of bread." Still later we see Mr. Fagin sitting "in the old den . . . brooding over a dull, smoky fire." And, then, the same image, but with a slight variation. Noah Claypole is sleeping on the floor.

Towards him the old man sometimes directed his eyes for an instant, and then brought them back again to the candle; which with a longburnt wick drooping almost double, and hot grease falling down in clots upon the table, plainly showed that his thoughts were busy else-where.

There is another of those candles at Krook's Rag and Bottle

Shop in *Bleak House* when Mr. Snagsby conducts Mr. Tulkinghorn thither in search of Mr. Nemo. They find him dead.

> He has a yellow look in the spectral darkness of a candle that has guttered down, until the whole length of its wick (still burning) has doubled over, and left a tower of winding-sheet above it.

Mr. Krook's spontaneous combustion is at the center of the cooking fire imagery. When Esther Summerson first sees him the breath "is issuing in visible smoke from his mouth, as if he were on fire within." Again when Messrs. Guppy and Weevle treat him to a renewed bottle of gin his "hot breath seems to come towards them like a flame."

And of course Fagin's "hot grease falling down in clots upon the table" occurs again on Krook's birthday when he cooks himself altogether into the circumambient greasy fog. Mild Mr. Snagsby sniffs him in the air, and tastes him in the air, and spits him out. He mildly objects to Mr. Weevle's suggestion that the smell is due to chops cooking at Sol's Arms. If that's it, they weren't quite fresh and the cook should be looked to. Krook falls in clots of hot grease, as black soot, as gobbets of black fat. He rains down upon Guppy and Weevle, who are waiting for him, in the form of thick yellow offensive smelly sticky liquid, and collects in nauseous pools. Krook is a slightly displaced representative of the evils and abuses of the Court of Chancery, which provides the major central theme for the novel. His spontaneous combustion thus described constitutes a marvelously, sickly hilarious rendition of the way in which Chancery poisons and pollutes the lives of all whom it touches.

Cooking fire is part and parcel of Krook's family. When

we are introduced to his relative by marriage, Grand-father Smallweed, he is by the fire near the trivets, the pots, and the kettles, and the "sort of brass gallows for roasting." Here he watches the fire and the roasting and the boiling. Mr. George observes that he is hot and commends his wisdom is getting used to it ahead of time. Again and again he is by the fire in one location or another.

The cooking fire train of associations, like the boiling liquid one, finds a modest but distinct expression in Mr. Venus, too. When Silas Wegg first goes to see Mr. Venus, he goes through the dark greasy entry and the little greasy dark door into the greasy little dark shop, all rendered greasy, presumably, by Mr. Venus' occasional need in his profession to boil the bones to get the meat off. Mr. Venus cooks people. It is human grease, at any rate, like Krook's. Such cooking makes the air greasy in much the same way Krook did.

By the dim light of one tallow candle Wegg sees the face of a man stooping low in a chair. "His expression and stoop are like those of a shoemaker," interestingly enough, but that is not what he is. His face, like Fagin's, is "sur-rounded by a tangle of reddish-dusty hair," and, to under-score the association, Mr. Venus provides for Mr. Wegg's refreshment by plucking the "arrow out of the breast of Cock Robbin" and toasting a muffin for him at the fire. Mr. Venus clearly shares certain essential qualities with the man, Fagin, the father, *the* progenitor, whom Oliver Twist saw engaged as the primary actor in the first enact-ment in the novels of the self-creating primal scene. He is, like Jenny Wren, someone who partakes of the nature of the ravager of the pure child, and he is like Fagin some-one who plays with the golden trinkets in the box taken from the secret hole.

Before we leave cooking fires and turn to other attri-

butes of these characters, there is still another parallel
train of associations I wish to mention. They are an offshoot
from cooking fires and have to do with beacon fires and
dark flickering fire-light illumination. In *Little Dorrit*
there is another toasting-fork and it is in Affery Flintwinch's hand:

> . . . the scorched countenance of Affery, who, with the
> kitchen toasting-fork still in her hand, looked like a sort
> of allegorical personage. . . .

This scene occurs in the bedroom of Mrs. Clennam, whom
Affery serves, and whose room is a kind of beacon:

> The varying light of fire and candle in Mrs. Clennam's
> room made the greatest change that ever broke the dead
> monotony of the spot. In her two long narrow windows,
> the fire shone sullenly all day, and sullenly all night.
> On rare occasions, it flashed up passionately, as she did;
> but for the most part it was suppressed, like her, and
> preyed upon itself evenly and slowly. Strange, if the little
> sickroom fire were in effect a beacon fire, summoning
> someone, and that the most unlikely someone in the
> world, to the spot that *must* be come to.

It is only from a superficial point of view that that someone
appears to be most unlikely. He is the incarnation of evil
in the novel, truly a satanic figure. He is the incarnation
of the idea of evil which fills Mrs. Clennam's mind and
marks the limit and focus of her twisted, distorted, love-
suppressing religiosity. It is in fact inevitable and natural
that he should come to her. It is natural that he should
come to blackmail her, for he is the incarnation of her
guilt as well as of her idea of evil. In the unconscious
mind one derives one's idea of evil from one's own sense

of guilt. It is inevitable that his coming should bring down
the House of Clennam, and it is altogether fitting that the
fall of that house should also smash him. Dickens makes
him more interesting and important by placing him among
those very special characters who have many names, or
sometimes, none. His name, variously, is Rigaud or Lag-
nier, or Blandois.

John Jasper operates a similar kind of lighthouse in the
Mystery of Edwin Drood. When the Dean and Minor
Canon Crisparkle and the rest look toward Jasper's win-
dows they see

> through its latticed window, a fire shines out upon the
> fast-darkening scene, involving in shadow the pendent
> masses of ivy and creeper covering the building's front.

Later Septimus Crisparkle calls on Jasper to persuade him
to burn the diary in which he recorded his fear that Neville
Landless threatened the life of "Ned" Drood. The Rev.
Mr. Crisparkle finds Jasper asleep by his fire. Still later
Jasper's only preparation for going out to make a night
of it is to sit at his piano chanting choir music by the hour
with no light but the fire. On the Christmas Eve when
Drood disappears, we observe that, as seen from the outside, "the red light burns steadily all the evening in the
lighthouse on the margin of the tide of busy life." Through
the terrible wind storm the red light in Jasper's window
burned on steadily. And like Mrs. Clennam's window
summoning Rigaud to death, presumably it lights Ned
Drood to his grave.

John Jasper is, in other words, via this tenuous route
back through Mrs. Clennam and Affery, connected, however remotely, with Fagin and Quilp and the goblin king.

We shall see that he is associated with them in other ways as well.

Meanwhile we should note another association of scenes. Like Mr. Krook in *Bleak House,* Peg Slideskew in *Nicholas Nickleby* is in possession of an important Will she cannot read, and like him, she seeks help in an effort to read it.

> The old woman, with her wrinkled face close to the bars of the stove, puffing at the dull embers which had not yet caught the wood; Squeers, stooping down to the candle, which brought out the full ugliness of his face, as the light of the fire did that of his companion; both intently engaged, and wearing faces of exultation. . . .

Like Mr. Nemo, who lived in Krook's house in *Bleak House,* John Jasper is addicted to opium. When we are first introduced to John Jasper by seeing the world through his eyes, we see him seeing the Princess Puffer, Jasper's chief purveyor of opium, fixing another pipe for him:

> And as she blows, shading it with her lean hand, concentrates its red spark of light, it serves in the dim morning as a lamp to show him what he sees of her.

This is a special kind of beacon light. Like Peg and Squeers, Jasper here is using the dim, blown-upon light to see something by. Here there is a difference, however, because the Princess Puffer is actually a part of Jasper, and the significance of this opening scene is that in the light of the opium he is revealing a part of himself to himself and to us. A short while later on in the novel Edwin Drood is astonished by his uncle's declaration that

he hates his own life, for all that it appears to be filled with
quiet and beauty and music. Jasper tell him:

> The echoes of my own voice among the arches seem to
> mock me with my daily drudging round. No wretched
> monk who droned his life away in that gloomy place,
> before me, can have been more tired of it than I am. He
> could take for relief (and did take) to carving demons
> out of the stalls and seats and desks. What shall I do?
> Must I take to carving them out of my heart?

That is, to be sure, just exactly what he does do. Much
later one of the gargoyles comes looking for him and finds
him. It is Her Royal Highness, the Princess Puffer and
Dick Datchery and Deputy Winks (who gave her that
name) watch her watching Jasper.

> She is behind a pillar, carefully withdrawn from the
> Choirmaster's view, but regards him with the closest
> attention. All unconscious of her presence, he chants and
> sings. She grins when he is most musically fervid, and—
> yes, Mr. Datchery sees her do it!—shakes her fist at him
> behind the pillar's friendly shelter.
>   Mr. Datchery looks again, to convince himself. Yes,
> again! As ugly and withered as one of the fantastic
> carvings on the under brackets of the stall seats, as malig-
> nant as the Evil One, as hard as the big brass eagle
> holding the sacred books upon his wings . . . she hugs
> herself in her lean arms, and then shakes both fists at
> the leader of the Choir.
>   And at that moment, outside the grated door of the
> Choir, having eluded the vigilance of Mr. Tope by shifty
> resources in which he is an adept, Deputy peeps, sharp-
> eyed, through the bars, and stares astounded from the
> threatener to the threatened.

It is very important in this novel to notice who is noticing whom. Dickens mentions that sort of thing quite often, and is very precise and exact about it here, as he almost always is in matters of importance to him. Dickens is here, as befits his genius, anticipating Henry James and his disciples. He has written a novel of which some of the action, and most of the unravelling, depend upon determining his point of view. These are almost the last paragraphs of *Edwin Drood* that Dickens wrote before he died. We do not in fact know how Dickens would have continued or finished it. Before he died Dickens had made only the most guarded and enigmatic hints about the conclusion of the novel even to so close a lifelong friend and editor as John Forster. But it is a reasonable supposition that Dickens had in mind bringing about a remarkable climax to the book. One half of Jasper's mind would be dissociated from the whole and would accuse himself of the crime of murdering his nephew Edwin Drood. The murderous half of his mind had been acting on the mistaken assumption that that would help him accomplish the union with Rosa Bud that he so ardently and compulsively desires. This is very much after the manner of Quilp's desire for Little Nell.

The dissociation between the two parts of Jasper would be related to his drug habit. The one person most intimately connected with that activity, and the one witness to his mutterings during opium-induced sleep, is naturally the Princess Puffer. John Jasper is "all unconscious of her presence" because she is in some sense his unconscious mind. She is therefore quite naturally in a position to accuse him of whatever it may be he is guilty of or at least thinks in a part of his mind he may be guilty of. The glow of the opium lump in the pipe the Princess Puffer puffs is another of those beacon fires. Like the fire in Jasper's study it may be beckoning Ned Drood to his death. It is at any rate intimately associated with that aspect of Jasper which plots murder and therefore constitutes the node or focus of evil in him. In the case of Jasper this person is clearly a part of the character of John Jasper himself. It is inside him.

In *A Tale of Two Cities* the wicked, or at any rate dissolute guilty part of the self, Sydney Carton, is put into a separate character from the good self, Charles Darnay. There is guilt associated with Darnay's *family,* but it does not personally attach itself to him. Nor do Sydney Carton's qualities attach to him for all that Carton looks exactly like Darnay and for all that wicked self Carton has to die so that good self Darnay can live. Carton has to have his head cut off, so as to enable his exact look-alike Darnay, to lie in bed with the girl he loves too, and experience an orgasm inside her.

It is getting a bit ahead of ourselves here to mention it, but we have already seen that Rigaud is a kind of incarnation of the wickedness which Mrs. Clennam regards as being the very nature of evil. She blames much of this on Arthur Clennam and also regards it as being her own focus of evil guilt in *Little Dorrit.* The wicked son or self, Rigaud, has to be destroyed, by a blow to the head not unlike the guillotine blow to Carton's neck, before the good self, or son, Arthur Clennam, can be redeemed and rewarded, released from prison, like Darnay, and, like Darnay, enabled to be married. The girl he marries, Little Dorrit, in addition to being in many other ways a reincarnation of Little Nell, actually fulfills for Clennam the role of daughter. In John Jasper's case, however, it is the drug together with the person, the Princess Puffer, who expose him to his own mind, or, at any rate, a part of it. It is the part where the demons are carved.

CHAPTER IV

THE OLDEST LETTUCE

Erotic Umbrellas and
Sexually Suggestive Food

THERE ARE OTHER ASSOCIATIONS binding together this group of characters linked by boiling liquids and beacon fires. One of the chief among them is laughter. The relationship of what makes laughter to what make dreams is a very large and complex subject. Freud talks about the whole domain of verbal wit being put at the disposal of the dream-work. Dreams are often amusing because the same kind of mechanism which gives meaning in dreams in a way sufficiently roundabout as to be permissible for expression is employed by the expert in verbal wit. Freud points out that dreams are often most profound when they seem most crazy or amusing. They use the same principle that is used by the Fool in a royal court when he acts the part of a buffoon by uttering truths no one else would dare to mention.

Just as Dickens' own idiosyncratic creative processes in his novels greatly resemble the unconscious ideation which seems to produce dreams, so Dickens' own idiosyncratic comic genius may in part be understood on an analogous basis. Dickens himself may have had some insight into the nature of laughter. It occurs as a sudden discharge of energy theretofore repressed. It is released by wit which allows earlier, infantile, unconscious modes of thinking to force themselves through into consciousness. Dickens does at any rate seem to exhibit such a thing in the wild and uncontrollable laughter which forms such a distinctive part of the emotional *repertoire* of the group of characters otherwise connected by the drinking of boiling liquids, or by cooking or beacon fires.

It is as Gabriel Grub's goblin laughs uproariously, writhing and whooping, that the other goblins appear. They come leaping into the church-yard in *Pickwick,* playing leap-frog with the tombstones while the first goblin, their king, plays leap-frog with the family vaults and tombs when he's not standing on his head on the point of his sugarloaf hat.

Charley Bates in *Oliver Twist* indulges in this kind of laughter. For dream purposes he is an offshoot from, or appendage to, Fagin, who is himself in the goblin family. Daniel Quilp, a direct descendant of the goblin king, rolls on the ground in an ecstacy of uncontrollable laughter at fooling Swiveller in the *Old Curiosity Shop* and at seeing Kit in custody. In the same novel it is true that young Kit Nubbles becomes a fairly straightforward young romantic "lead," on the usual Dickensian model, unheroic, snobbish, and rather self-centered and unhumorous. But at the beginning of the novel, before Nell and her grandfather run away from London, he was something of a grotesque himself. He had the ability to laugh and to arouse laughter in others that is, in its way, reminiscent of Charley Bates in *Oliver Twist,* and prospective of Sloppy in *Our Mutual Friend.* During his early direct association with Nell, he is the kind of goblinesque gargoyle with which she is characteristically surrounded. It is only when she is physically removed from him that he no longer has to fulfill that necessary function for her and so he can drop that aspect of his nature.

This tells us a great deal about Nell and Quilp and their world. To know Nell is to love her. To know Nell's caritative pure spirit is to desire her erotically. Nell's caritative loving nature is almost pure spirit. Quilp's erotic force is almost unrelieved earthiness. As long as Nell is alive she is forever surrounded by earthiness. Quilp is, in other words, all around Nell all the time until she dies to escape him. Quilp is the most powerful incarnation in the book of a principle, the goblin principle, which pervades the earth. Anything earthy which perceives Nell's goodness and beauty desires to invade it erotically. The greater her caritative goodness, the stronger the erotic desire. The earthy erotic desire expresses itslf in goblin form. Thus Quilp, who desires Nell *most,* is the king of the goblins in the *Old Curiosity Shop.*

There are many lesser goblins who surround Nell wherever she goes, from the gargoyles in the Old Curiosity Shop, to Codlin and Short's Punch and Judy among the gravestones, to Mrs. Jarley's waxworks and the midnight arch through which Quilp comes like a statue from a niche, to the fire watchers of England's industrial hell, and at last to the church full of tombs, statues and gargoyles which surround Little Nell when she dies. The goblins appear among the tombs in the graveyard because they are its essence: dead clay, the element of earth. They laugh uproariously at death because they cannot be made more dead, more earthy, more claylike than they already are.

Goblin laughter can be heard in *Barnaby Rudge,* principally when Barnaby's bird Grip makes him laugh that kind of laugh. If you take the two together, the mentally retarded son of the murderer everyone thinks is dead but who is actually around to haunt churchyards at night, and his familiar spirit the raven, they do constitute rather a goblinlike symbiosis. In the same novel Sim Tappertit makes Hugh laugh that kind of laugh. While Hugh clearly has goblin qualities, Sim's nocturnal underground secret apprentice society is at least superficially goblinesque. Both Sim and Hugh, of course, entertain for Dolly Varden the same kind of desire Quilp has for Nell.

Major Bagstock in *Dombey and Son* has goblin qualities and his fits of laughter come close to killing him each time, but, alas, not quite successfully. Mostly it is the men who have such laughing fits, but Estella laughs *too much* at the thought of Pip's causing torment to Miss Havisham's jealous relations in *Great Expectations.* Fascination Fledgeby laughs that way silently in *Our Mutual Friend,* and so does Jasper in *Drood,* while he watches Crisparkle and Landless, and is watched, in turn, by Durdles.

It is worth reminding the reader that what established the association is the simple propinquity of occurrence. These groups of people reveal the similarities in their hidden identities and qualities in the first instance by the fact that the same images or actions are associated with them. It is the simultaneity of occurrence in time which makes the connection in nonlogical unconscious thinking.

If there were no other way of identifying Daniel Quilp as a reincarnation of the goblin king, one could do so from the fact that Tom Scott, Quilp's familiar spirit, is so often seen standing on his head, just like the goblin. It is upon the point of his sugarloaf hat that the goblin king stands.

Among the other ways in which he tortures Grub, the goblin uses the taper corner of the hat to poke Gabriel's eyes "thereby occasioning him the most exquisite pain." This hat appears again much later, without the goblin himself, but still associated with the fiery hot liquor that the goblin drinks. The Six Jolly Fellowship-Porters, the primary waterfront drinking place in *Our Mutual Friend,* specializes in hot drinks, mulled ale, purl, flip, dog's nose, and other hot toddies. They are expertly made in those "fireside tin utensils, like models of sugarloaf hats" with "pointed ends" to put down "in the depth of the red coals." This is the sort of thing Eugene Wrayburn and Mortimer Lightwood and Mr. Inspector sit all night drinking while waiting to arrest Gaffer Hexam.

If there were no other evidence to connect the goblin king with John Jasper, one might do so from the fact that the only two wicker bottles mentioned in all fifteen novels bring them together. It is out of a wicker bottle that Gabriel Grub drinks the powerful liquor that introduces him to his Rip Van Winkleish encounter with the goblins among the graves in *Pickwick.* It is out of the other wicker bottle that John Jasper supplies the hocussed liquor Stoney Durdles drinks that puts him into the long sleep in the Cathedral crypt while Jasper is up to his goblin tricks among the tombs of *Edwin Drood.*

There is another oddly trivial simultaneity of association which further links Fagin, Venus, and Jenny Wren together. In *Oliver Twist* Bill Sikes says Fagin is a curiosity of ugliness fit only to be preserved as such in a glass bottle. In the *Old Curiosity Shop* Kit Nubbles makes a similar remark when he says Quilp is an uglier dwarf than

you can see anywhere for a penny. In *Our Mutual Friend*
Mr. Venus has a "Hindoo baby in a bottle, curved up with
his big head tucked under him, as though he would instantly throw a summersault if the bottle were large
enough." A goblin summersault for a goblin baby in a
bottle.

We have already seen that Mr. Venus is descended, however indirectly, from Mr. Fagin and Mr. Krook and Mr.
Quilp. Here, also, we see that Jenny Wren, in addition to
the other qualities she shares with Daniel Quilp, remarks
of her alcoholic father that he is "a muddling and a swipey
old child . . . fit for nothing but to be preserved in the
liquor that destroys him, and put in a great glass bottle
as a sight for other swipey children of his own pattern."
The association is, again, underscored by the fact that there
are no other curiosities in bottles in the novels.

David Copperfield's friend James Steerforth, who
drowns once, is linked with "our mutual friend's" poisoner,
Roger Riderhood, who drowns twice. The simple insignificant detail that unites them is that they are the only two
characters in all of Dickens' novels who drink out of foot-
less glasses. In the afterhours parties at Salem House,
Steerforth uses a little glass without a foot to drink the
current wine provided by David Copperfield's funds. It is
from a glass without a foot that Riderhood drinks the
sherry wine provided by the mysterious visitor wearing
George Radfoot's clothing.

Choirmaster Jasper and lawyer Jaggers are both men
who are talented in the exercise of almost hypnotic influence to stimulate the baser passions of those around
them and to manipulate them. At the conclusion of an
altercation Jaggers has instigated in *Great Expectations,*
Bentley Drummle is about to hurl a heavy glass at the
head of his colleague Startop. Jaggers seizes the glass at

the last moment. At the conclusion of a nearly identical incident in *Drood,* Neville Landless, in an anger largely created and fostered by John Jasper, is about to hurl a glass at Edwin Drood's head. Jasper, who has had control all the time, stops him at the last moment by catching Neville's arm.

Grandfather Smallweed, who also throws things and sits by the fire, cannot leave his chair and is carried about *Bleak House* everywhere in it. He is the resident spirit of the chair. He is a reincarnation of the chair which turns out to be an ugly old man in *Pickwick,* who winks and grins at Tom Smart "like a superannuated monkey." Like Smallweed, he is a discoverer of vital papers.

When one becomes fully accustomed to the workings of this language of association by the simultaneity of props, one can readily perceive the importance of the description of what Silas Wegg observes in Mr. Venus' shop window when he first meets him and introduces him to the reader. It is a

dark shop-window with a tallow candle dimly burning in it, surrounded by a muddle of objects, vaguely resembling pieces of leather and dry stick, but among which nothing is resolvable into anything distinct, save the candle itself in its old tin candle-stick, and two preserved frogs fighting a small-sword duel.

The importance of this very unusual prop in *Our Mutual Friend* is that its other occurrence was on Dickens' own desk, where, when he was working, he was habitually surrounded by certain familiar objects. These included a French bronze casting of a seller of little dogs, a rabbit sitting on a leaf, a huge paperknife, a little cup of fresh flowers, the daily register of the month and day of the week, and, last but not least, a bronze casting of a pair of duelling frogs. And so we learn a highly significant aspect of Mr. Venus' identity. In addition to representing Quilp and Fagin, he is connected with the author himself. This is especially interesting when you reflect that Mr. Venus did for Silas Wegg's leg what Bella Wilfer did for old Gruff and Glum's. But more of this later.

Meanwhile we may profitably find other traces of the author's identity revealed in the props. To do so we may first observe some relations among three other props; noses, clocks, and toothpicks. Nose pulling is particularly offensive, whether it seems to refer to castration or to masturbation. The outstanding instance in the novels is Lammle intimidating Fledgeby in *Our Mutual Friend* by offering to pull his nose: "Give me your nose, sir!" He doesn't do it, but the call is close, and inspires Fledgeby to pull Pubsey and Co.'s nose:

> Fledgeby . . . pulled the house-bell as if it were the house's nose. . . . he angrily pulled the house's nose again, and pulled and pulled and continued to pull, until a human nose appeared in the dark doorway.

That the nature of the insult is similar is clear in *Dombey and Son* when we see vicious Robin Toodle, upon deserting Captain Cuttle.

> going out upon the door-step, pulled the little Midshipman's nose as a parting indignity, and went away down the street grinning triumph.

Daniel Quilp is naturally outstanding among Dickens' fictional sadists. The wooden ship's figurehead admiral stands for Kit Nubbles in the *Old Curiosity Shop* in the same way the little Wooden Midshipman stands for Walter Gay in *Dombey and Son*. Quilp not only sears the face of this huge wooden effigy with a red-hot poker, but also inserts a tenpenny nail in the tip of the figure's nose.

Daniel Quilp performs this act of voodooism in his waterside countinghouse. It is here in this office that he has the clock which he hasn't wound for a long time and from which he has twisted the minute hand to use as a toothpick. Toothpicks quite consistently express arrogance and insolence in the novels. Sir Mulberry Hawk of *Nicholas Nickleby,* Sir John Chester in *Barnaby Rudge,* and literally two-faced Zephaniah Scadder of *Martin Chuzzlewit* are outstandingly memorable for their toothpickmanship, but toothpicks convey insult virtually wherever they appear. That Quilp's insult to this clock is especially vicious is made partly clear by the fact that clocks, like other machinery and apparatus, sometimes stand, in dreams, for the genitals, and generally the male ones. It is made further clear by the fact that clocks, like dueling frogs, seem to suggest the identity of the author.

In a letter to his friend Forster, Dickens wrote the following about the genesis of the *Old Curiosity Shop*:

I have a notion of this old file in the queer house opening the book by an account of himself, and, among his other peculiarities, of his affection for an old quaint queer-cased clock. . . . Then I mean to tell how that he has kept odd manuscripts in the old, deep, dark, silent closet where the weights are; and taken them from thence to read. . . . And thus I shall call the book either Old Humphrey's Clock, or Master Humphrey's Clock.

It is Master Humphrey who introduces us to Little Nell, but it is the clock which provides him with his stories; in other words, it is the author. That Dickens himself evidently had some insight into the workings of the unconscious in connection with his own creative activity is suggested by the fact that the specific part of the clock where the manuscripts originate is "the old, deep, dark, silent closet where the weights are." It is, in short, that place which is obscure and impenetrable to the conscious mind, where memory helps bring forth manuscripts.

Clocks seem further associated not only with the author himself, but with the father figure. Sometimes it seems to be the author's father; sometimes it is the author *as* father. It is at that level of unconscious thought where the male psyche identifies itself with the father, and especially with his genitals, while he is at the same time in conflict with him for the sexual object. The boy wants to be in his father's place, and so the boy's genitals and his father's genitals appear to be the same genitals. We shall find this situation recurring in other ways.

Daniel Quilp pops out like a figure in a Dutch clock upon Mrs. Nubbles and the Single Gentleman after their abortive pursuit of Nell in the *Old Curiosity Shop*. And Quilp, we recall, is a kind of father to Nell, to the Marchioness, and to Dick Swiveller, who sees him in fantasy as the progenitive organs.

In *Martin Chuzzlewit* Jonas tells Pecksniff that the noise means there is something wrong in the clock. It turns out to be his father's death rattle as he runs down and stops. In *Little Dorrit* "There was the large, hard-featured clock in the sideboard" which Arthur Clennam used to see

bending its figured brows upon him with a savage joy when he was behindhand with his lessons, and which, when it was wound up once a week with an iron handle, used to sound as if it were growling in ferocious anticipation of the miseries into which it would bring him.

Just as the manuscripts come out of Master Humphrey's clocks, there is in *Great Expectations,* in one of the plays in which Wopsle acts, the part of an honest little grocer. He gets into a clock with a grid-iron, overhears certain key conversations, and emerges to set the plot straight like the author-surrogate *deus ex machina* he clearly is. And in the same novel, Pip's pseudo-father Abel Magwitch has a characteristic way of showing he's deeply moved by making a click in his throat "as if he had works in him like a clock, and was going to strike."

There are strong indications here, at any rate, that an assault upon a clock, like Quilp's, for example, points by association to some kind of symbolic molestation of the father's genitals. If one needed any closer link between Quilp and Jasper, it is provided by the fact that on that fateful Christmas Eve when Edwin Drood disappears, the wind storm is so violent it tears the hands off the Cathedral clock. John Jasper, of course, is also "Jack." And the Cathedral clock is up in a high tower, like the tower the newly married Rokesmith's headwaiter climbed. Or, at a slightly further remove, like the beanstalk Jack climbed.

Finally, in *Our Mutual Friend,* upon arriving at Nicodemus Boffin's house to apply Noddy's nose to the grindstone—and Mr. Boffin is a father-surrogate to both Bella Wilfer and John Harmon—The "all powerful Wegg wore his hat, and whistled, and with his forefinger stirred up a clock that stood upon the chimney-piece, until he made it strike." This brings us back to the interesting consideration of Wegg's identity.

I have already developed at some length the associations which point to the hidden identities within Jenny Wren and

Mr. Venus. Both are in part symbolic expressions of the person with the compulsion to violate the pure child. That person is perhaps somewhat more prominent in Jenny than in Venus, but he is there in both. In Venus, moreover, there is a further indication quite clearly that the sinister father playing with the golden trinkets from the box in the secret hole is present, and, interestingly, in association with the identity of the author.

We already know enough about Silas Wegg to suspect that he is an expression of the negative, denying aspect of the father. His role in the novel expresses this quite explicitly, because he does become a resident in old Harmon's old house. Although he is there in terms of the plot's secondary revision only as a caretaker, he is at a deeper level there as a representative of mean old Mr. Harmon himself (whose other primary incarnation, or haunting, in the novel is as old Gruff and Glum). While there his whole line of action consists of efforts to hurt the good, positive, affirming, loving aspect of the father, Noddy Boffin, and to deprive the son, John Harmon, of his inheritance of golden refuse. His function is similar to that of Barkis or old Bill Barley with respect to the gold which represents food, and, sometimes, represents the girl symbolically. This is particularly true in this novel because the girl and the gold are uniquely and intimately linked together in and by the father's Will.

Wegg's wooden leg also relates him associatively to Bill Barley whose growl in the beam sounds like the threatening attack of a giant wooden leg from upstairs. Wegg's wooden leg is a symbolic representation of the progenitive phallus, but it also represents a deprivation of that phallus, a castration. We know these things already about Wegg, and it is interesting to see them further borne out by other props as well.

There are a great many umbrellas in Dickens' novels just as there are in real life. While umbrellas in dreams often represent the phallus, (erect when the umbrella is opened), they are certainly in that category of props which most often ought to be taken just at face value. Nevertheless, in some instances the umbrellas in Dickens' novels do seem representative of sexual imagery in a symbolic and, often, comic way. The red-nosed shepherd in *Pickwick,* Mr. Stiggins, who is Tony Weller's second wife's rather dilapidated other interest, has a green umbrella that is falling apart with the whalebone coming out at the bottom. It suffers also the lack of a handle. Elsewhere in the same novel, as an instance of political corruption and rank bribery for votes during the Eatanswill election, Mr. Perker, who is candidate Slumkey's agent, tells Pickwick:

"We had a little tea-party here, last night—five-and-forty women, my dear sir—and gave every one of 'em a green parasol when she went away."

"A parasol!" said Mr. Pickwick.

"Fact, my dear sir, Fact. Five-and-forty green parasols, at seven and sixpence a-piece. All women like finery,—extraordinary the effect of those parasols. Secured all their husbands, and half their brothers—beats stockings, and flannel, and all that sort of thing hollow. My idea, my dear sir, entirely. Hail, rain, or sunshine, you can't walk a dozen yards up the street, without encountering half a dozen green parasols."

Near the end of the novel when Pickwick encounters ruined, despondent, and reformed Jingle in the Fleet Prison, he is amazed to learn that he "lived for three weeks upon a pair of boots, and a silk umbrella with an ivory handle!" It is hard to fail to read into this precise choice of objects to hock symbolic reference to Jingle's present downfall and former erotic prowess.

The Infant Phenomenon in *Nicholas Nickleby* carries a green parasol with a broad fringe border and no handle that gets dropped down an iron grating. Later in the same novel the umbrella with which Mr. Lillyvick signals his devotion to Miss Petowker is a green cotton one with a battered ferule. And later again, when Nicholas masterminds his mother in an exodus away from Uncle Ralph Nickleby's premises—and Uncle Ralph certainly represents another, negative, denying, symbolic father-figure—she thinks she remembers leaving a green umbrella behind some unknown door. And in *David Copperfield,* Clara Copperfield's old parasol frayed the whole way up with a mangy fringe is also a green one, just before she meets Murdstone.

There are two blue umbrellas (one's a parasol, actually), and one lilac parasol, Miss Monflathers', in the *Old Curiosity Shop,* which really doesn't count. The blue parasol is carried by a lady Nell sees in a decorative tea-tray. In *Dombey and Son* Captain Cuttle hires "the daughter of an elderly lady, who usually sat under a blue umbrella in Leadenhall Market, selling Poultry" to come look after Florence.

The umbrella picture, in other words, is a predominantly green one with one touch of blue in it, and that is exactly a description of Mrs. Gamp's umbrella in *Martin Chuzzlewit*:

> Mrs. Gamp had . . . a species of gig umbrella . . . in colour like a faded leaf, except where a circular patch of a lively blue had been dexterously let in at the top.

Sarah Gamp's umbrella is, in fact, among the symbolic props, *the* archetypal umbrella. It is, furthermore, an elongated object which is, for most of its length, one color, but which at the end becomes another color, a fairly graphic displaced representation of a phallus with the glans penis at the end. We shall see that Mrs. Gamp's umbrella is *the* archetypal phallus in the novels. That this is indeed what it symbolizes is made clear in the following passage:

It was a troublesome matter to adjust Mrs. Gamp's luggage to her satisfaction; for every package belonging to that lady had the inconvenient property of requiring to be put in a boot by itself, and to have no other luggage near it, on pain of actions at law for heavy damages against the proprietors of the coach. The umbrella with the circular patch was particularly hard to be got rid of, and several times thrust out its battered brass nozzle from improper crevices and chinks, to the great terror of the other passengers. Indeed, in her intense anxiety to find a haven of refuge for this chattel, Mrs. Gamp so often moved it, in the course of five minutes, that it seemed not one umbrella but fifty. At length it was lost, or said to be; and for the next five minutes she was face to face with the coachman, go wherever he might, protesting that it should be "made good," though she took the question to the House of Commons.

This is a wonderful comic, symbolic, displaced fantasy of the Dickens primal scene, the progenitive act of sexual intercourse between the parents. For of course *Martin Chuzzlewit,* for a novel all about conflict between fathers and sons, is conspicuously lacking in mothers, except for Mrs. Gamp. She cannot be brought into too close proximity with any of the fathers, and especially not with the major father figures, old Martin himself and Mr. Pecksniff. She is

Mrs. Gamp: Her Umbrella and Bonnet

kept at a distance from them. They are provided with wives who are long dead before the novel begins.

Mrs. Gamp is provided with a husband, who had a wooden leg, who is also dead before the novel begins. This is partly for the purposes of concealment which the censorship requires. It is partly also because, as we shall more and more clearly see throughout the remainder of this book, Dickens' unconscious sexual mythology tends to keep opposites, including sexually paired opposites, apart and frustrated in the earlier novels. It tends to bring them closer and closer together toward fulfillment in the later novels, however, a fact essential to the understanding of *Our Mutual Friend* and of Bella Wilfer's wedding to John Rokesmith.

The dead and buried wooden legged Mr. Gamp serves another function, too. He represents an aspect of the father for which neither Pecksniff nor old Martin are suited, and that is that the mother has castrated the father. Like Martha Varden, the mother symbolized in Mrs. Gamp is a castrating woman. Unlike Martha Varden she is unredeemed. Her husband went to his grave wooden legged, and she keeps the phallus she took from him in her possession. Wherever she goes, she must have "the indispensable umbrella, without which neither a lying-in nor a laying-out could by any possibility be attempted." Observe the puns, and, observe that the object unites the ideas of birth and death. In Mrs. Gamp's bedroom we see her "umbrella, which as something of great price and rarity, was displayed with particular ostentation."

Indeed, there is a great deal of sexual imagery surrounding Mrs. Gamp, especially in her bedroom. I don't wish to appear to apply the sexual myth of the Loathly Hag in any rigid or insistent way to Dickens' novels, because it does not apply equally well to them all. But it does provide useful insight when applied to *Martin Chuzzlewit,* because there are two women in the novel who are surrounded by the same kind of sexual imagery. One is loathly, Mrs. Gamp, the other is quite cute, Ruth Pinch. Cherry and Merry Pecksniff are conventionally and superficially sexy or not sexy as the occasions of the plot require. Mary Graham, the central erotic object of the novel, who is in possession of one father, old Martin, wooed by the other father, Pecksniff, and loved by two of the three primary sons, young Martin, who finally gets her, and Tom Pinch who doesn't,—Mary is rendered almost completely in asexual terms. She is not demonstrated to be desirable in the least. Probably because her name *is* Mary the sexual interest truly invested in her has to be altogether repressed and transferred out to Ruth Pinch.

It is the case, of course, that the Loathly Hag situation with its *two* women can demonstrate the subtleties and complexities of the desire a great deal more explicitly than would be possible with a single figure. As we shall shortly see, much of the sexual imagery surrounding Ruth involves her brother, Tom, who ostensibly is hopelessly in love with Mary. Ruth is the displaced sexual object with whom Tom can flirt flagrantly but innocently. He is unable to invest Mary with sexual imagery both because of her name and because the repression of the sexual interest in Mary comes about because *she* is the *real sister* in the case. Ruth finally marries the third of the primary sons, John Westlock.

Mrs. Gamp, at any rate, for all that she is loathly, and, indeed, in one sense *because* she is loathly, inhabits a bedroom full of sexually symbolic images and objects. The sacking of her bed is so "low and bulgy" that "Mrs. Gamp's box would not go under it, but stopped half-way, in a manner which, while it did violence to the reason, likewise endangered the legs of a stranger." It is just like that box under Barkis' bed. The frame of Mrs. Gamp's bed "was ornamented with divers pippins carved in timber, which on the slightest provocation, and frequently on none at all, came tumbling down; harrassing the peaceful guest with inexplicable terrors." What one is terrorized by, of course, is the sexual significance of these things. There is a good deal more of the same, including a number of band-boxes whose idiosyncrasy was that "though every band box had a carefully closed lid, not one among them had a bottom," and a chest of drawers all the handles of which "had been long ago pulled off."

Mrs. Gamp and her umbrella have one rival and that is Mrs. Bagnet and *her* umbrella in *Bleak House*. She is another reincarnation of the castrating mother.

It is of no colour known in this life, and has a corrugated wooden crook for a handle, with a metallic object let into its prow or beak, resembling a little model of a fan-light over a street door, or one of the oval glasses out of a pair of spectacles: which ornamental object has not that tenacious capacity of sticking to its post that might be desired in an article long associated with the British Army. The old girl's umbrella is of a flabby habit of waist, and seems to be in need of stays—an appearance that is possibly referable to its having served, through a series of years, at home as a cupboard, and on journeys as a carpet bag. She never puts it up, having the greatest reliance on her well-proved cloak with its capacious hood, but generally uses the instrument as a wand with which to point out joints of meat or bunches of greens in marketing, or to arrest the attention of tradesmen by a friendly poke.

Mrs. Bagnet, like Mrs. Gamp, has symbolically taken her husband's phallus from him. She rules. He characteristically has no opinions or judgments about anything at all, and when asked for his opinion on any matter, invariably asks the old girl to say what it is that he thinks. He does not have a wooden leg. But he does have a wooden head. Indeed, his face is so wooden he is familarly known as "lignum vitae." The instrument thus torn from her husband no longer renders its original form of service inasmuch as "she never puts it up."

Mrs. Bagnet's umbrella sometimes points out joints of meat like phalluses, and sometimes bunches of greens like pubic hair. Mrs. Gamp's umbrella also appears in close association with analogous salad makings, partly through the agency of Mrs. Gamp herself, and partly through her alter ego, Betsey Prig. When Betsey comes to tea with Mrs. Gamp she brings with her a twopenny salad which she pulls out of her pocket and which includes

> a handful of mustard and cress, a trifle of the herb called dandelion, three bunches of radishes, an onion rather larger than an average turnip, three substantial slices of beetroot, and a short prong or antler of clergy. . . .

and the climax of which is

> . . . either the oldest of lettuces or youngest of cabbages, but at any rate, a green vegetable of an expansive nature, and of such magnificent proportions that she was obliged to shut it up like an umbrella before she could pull it out.

While "up" this enormous phallus so copiously covered with and surrounded by pubic hair could not be removed from her "pocket." She had to allow it to be shut up, that is, to detumesce, before it could come out. The situation occurs elsewhere in the same novel, in America, where Sarah Gamp's umbrella is reduplicated in Elijah Pogram's:

> The bell being rung for dinner at this moment, everybody ran away into the cabin, whither the Honourable Elijah Pogram fled with such precipitation that he forgot his umbrella was up, and fixed it so tightly in the cabin door that it could neither be let down nor got out.

Elijah Pogram's phallus appears to be in the hilariously worse predicament that it cannot be dislodged at all.

But Mrs. Gamp's umbrella, "in colour like a faded leaf," provides us with an interesting confirmation of the identity of Silas Wegg, because, when he is first introduced to us, it happens to be in his possession:

> When the weather was wet, he put up his umbrella over his stock-in-trade, not over himself; when the weather was dry, he furled that faded article, tied it round with a piece of yarn, and laid it crosswise under the trestles: where it looked like an unwholesomely-forced lettuce that had lost in colour and crispness what it had gained in size.

Silas Wegg here in *Our Mutual Friend* represents the man the mother castrated, just as Mr. Gamp does, but with the immensely significant difference that he has gotten back the phallus she took from him. It is still flaccid and useless, but he has got it back into his own possession again. To make such a symbolic situation entirely clear there is a back up system which makes the same statement and that is that he gets it back again from Mr. Venus. It is still useless as a leg, but he does have it back. A part of the significance of this for *Our Mutual Friend* can be seen in the fact that Silas Wegg's representative at Bella Wilfer's wedding, old Gruff and Glum with *two* wooden legs, does finally achieve a kind of miraculous erection, and, as we shall see, makes appropriate use of it as well.

In addition to the wooden leg and the umbrella, Silas Wegg reveals his family relationship with Mrs. Gamp in another way. Mrs Gamp is outstanding for her prodigality at throwing off wraiths, either in the form of clothing which retains her form even after she's taken it off, and, away from her, looks just like her, or in the form of fictitious characters. The chief among these is Mrs. Harris, who is not only a triumphant fictional creation herself, but actually brings into existence with her more than thirty other friends and relations hatched from the divine Sarah's fertile mind. So also is Wegg in part Gamp *redivivus* in his propensity for imagining the entire interior of "Our House" and filling it with fictional inmates like Miss Elizabeth, Master George, Aunt Jane, and Uncle Parker.

In addition to her big umbrella and capacity for self-reduplication, Mrs. Gamp has another idiosyncratic quality, and that is her quite extraordinary free-associative, stream-of-consciousness mode of discourse. There is nothing like it in English fiction until Molly Bloom, except, of course, for Mrs. Nickleby and Flora Finching, both of whom also talk in similar ways. It is obviously a quality associated in Dickens' novels with the idea of the mother.

In *Nicholas Nickleby* it seems clear that the loathly part of the hag is represented by Mrs. Nickleby herself, whose conversational style so nearly resembles Mrs. Gamp's whereas the young and attractive part is represented by Kate and Madeline. In *Little Dorrit* the situation is more interesting, and, as we have learned to expect in a later novel, it is more overtly revealing. For here the loathly part of the hag is Flora herself, while the attractive part consists partly of Minnie ("pet") Meagles and partly also of Flora herself as she was when she and Arthur Clennam were young and infatuated with each other. What is interesting is that Flora, at least to some extent, represents both parts. It is a much more interesting perception on Dickens' part that the same person is involved in both parts. It reiterates the identity which includes Little Em'ly, Dora Spenlow, and Clara Cooperfield.

In *Martin Chuzzlewit,* as I have indicated, the two parts of the loathly hag are to be found in Sarah Gamp and Ruth Pinch. But in order to exhibit Ruth Pinch's circumambient sexual imagery with the proper *éclat* we need first observe some of the significance of water.

In Dickens as in other writers, especially Victorian ones, and in dreams, water often unites death-dealing and birth-giving images and qualities. I shall be talking about this off and on the remainder of the book. It is very often expressive of rebirth in Dickens' fiction, and it is this sort of significance which it adumbrates at Bella's wedding to John Rokesmith:

> Stranded was Gruff and Glum in a harbour of everlasting mud, when all in an instant Bella floated him, and away he went.

And again, later on:

> It was a pleasant sight, in the midst of the golden bloom, to see this salt old Gruff and Glum waving his shovel hat at Bella, while his thin white hair flowed free, as if she had once more launched him into blue water again.

But it can exhibit other kinds of meaning, too.

When women holding watering cans in Dickens' novels

are found watering their flowers with them, it is invariably unrequited love which is expressed. In *Pickwick*, Mr. Tupman's declaration of love to Miss Wardle, who later runs off with Jingle, is made while she waters her flowers and it is interrupted by the inopportune arrival of the Fat Boy. In *Dombey and Son* Miss Tox is watering her plants as Mrs. Chick tells her of her brother Paul's engagement to Edith Granger. This ended Miss Tox's hopes, and while fainting away in Major Bagstock's Native's arms, she waters him too. In *Our Mutual Friend* Miss Peecher waters her flowers as she observes Bradley Headstone walking forth, and she contemplates the fact that he loves Lizzie Hexam and not herself.

From the earliest memory of man, rain, in dreams, mythology, or folklore, has signified, among other things, the fructifying copulation of the heavenly Father with the earth Mother. It is fairly commonplace in fiction for violent rain storms to be associated with violent scenes of passion. Dickens is not exceptional in this regard. But in Dickens' fiction the sexual passion involved is often guilty, and involves wrongdoing of some kind.

It is an endless torrential fall of snow and sleet which accompanies the long search for Esther's mother in *Bleak House*. Esther and Inspector Bucket and Allan Woodcourt find her dead at the foot of Esther's father's grave. The mode of this death is emblematic of the guilt underlying Esther's birth. In *Hard Times* there is a torrential downpour, a veritable flood, most of which falls on Mrs. Sparsit, when she thinks she has caught Louisa adulterously running off with Harthouse. In *David Copperfield*, it was the Copperfield neighbors, the Graypers, who introduced Clara to Murdstone, and so brought death and desolation to David's Garden of Eden. When the Graypers go off to South America, the rain makes its way through the roof of their empty house and stains the outer walls. Later in the same book the rain falls in a torrent when Little Em'ly runs off with Steerforth, and it is again torrential when Steerforth returns, drowned.

In *Bleak House* again it is only on one occasion that Esther Summerson actually causes the sound of the ghost walking on Chesney Wold's Ghost's Walk. She is, of course, the embodiment of the shameful guilt of that mansion's mistress. Usually it is the rain that makes the sound of the ghost walking there. And in *Our Mutual Friend* it is with a furious sweep of rain that Bradley Headstone rushes in at Riderhood's door "like the storm itself," so that his manner at once tells Riderhood: "You've seen him with her!" After Bradley's wrathfully orgiastic nosebleed, he goes out again into the rain to wash off his blood.

In the *Old Curiosity Shop* it is a heavy rain that forces Nell and her grandfather to shelter at the Valiant Soldier, and so fall in with Jowl and List. It is while the rain falls fast and furious outside that Nell's grandfather, in his compulsive gambling sickness, comes into Nell's bedroom at night to rob her of her last bit of money. Aside from the cribbage and Quilp's usurpation of Nell's bed, Grandfather Trent's theft of Nell's money from her bedroom while the rain pours down is the closest Dickens comes toward actually portraying sexual contact between Quilp and Nell. It is only through Quilp's representative, Grandfather Trent in the grip of his compulsion, and only using the symbolic theft of Nell's money, that Dickens can permit an adumbration of the rape of Nell.

It is in the form of fountains that water points with the most explicit sexuality to Ruth Pinch. In the courtyard of one of Miss Wade's Houses in *Little Dorrit,* where she is a kind of incarnation of passionate lovelessness, there is a dead wall, and a dead gateway. In the middle where there should have been a little statue, except that it is missing, there is also a little fountain that is completely dry. Elsewhere in that novel at the wedding of Edmund Sparkler and Fanny Dorrit:

> The choked old fountain, where erst the gladiators washed, might have leaped into life again to honour the ceremony.

It is perhaps Fanny's essential boredom with Mr. Sparkler that keeps the fountain dry. In *Great Expectations* Wemmick's bower during his courting days includes a fountain, and so does Bella Rokesmith Harmon's new home in *Our Mutual Friend*. But in *Martin Chuzzlewit* at Fountain Court where John Westlock daily comes to meet Ruth Pinch accidentally, and where their courtship prospers, the Temple Fountain is very explicit indeed:

> The Temple Fountain might have leaped up twenty feet to greet the spring of hopeful maidenhood, that in her person stole on, sparkling, through the dry and dusty channels of the Law.

That mountain continues leaping, plashing, splashing, and dancing throughout their courtship, and, at their marriage, it quenches old Fiery Face.

Aside from the excited fountain and the big butts of beer, the sexual character of Ruth's role is most clearly revealed in the one most intensely dramatized act she performs, the making of the beefsteak pudding. The whole scene is rendered in terms of her coquettishness with her brother, Tom, the same kind of behavior Bella Wilfer displays toward her father. The very setting is significant:

No doll's house ever yielded greater delight to its young mistress, than little Ruth derived from her glorious dominion over the triangular parlour and the two small bedrooms.

This triangular parlor with the two small bedrooms is clearly pelvic, boxlike, suggestive of the aperture between the two thighs, perhaps, or the triangular patch of pubic hair above and partly between the two legs. Ruth is, in any case, the keeper of Tom's house.

To be Tom's housekeeper. What dignity! Housekeeping, upon the commonest terms, associated itself with elevated responsibilities of all sorts and kinds; but housekeeping for Tom implied the utmost complication of grave trusts and mighty charges.

One does not have to be too skilled at punning, nor at the occurrence of verbal wit in unconscious ideation, to penetrate to the significance of those "elevated responsibilities," "grave trusts," and "mighty charges."

The making of the beefsteak pudding requires, first of all, the buying of a steak, and Tom and Ruth go together to attend to that necessary chore:

To see the butcher slap the steak, before he laid it on the block, and give his knife a sharpening, was to forget breakfast instantly. It was agreeable, too—it really was— to see him cut it off, so smooth and juicy. There was nothing savage in the act, although the knife was large and keen; it was a piece of art, high art; there was delicacy of touch, skilful handling of the subject, fine shading. It was the triumph of mind over matter; quite.

Perhaps the greenest cabbage-leaf ever grown in a

garden was wrapped about this steak, before it was delivered over to Tom. But the butcher had a sentiment for
his business, and knew how to refine upon it. When he
saw Tom putting the cabbage-leaf into his pocket awk-
wardly, he begged to be allowed to do it for him; "for
meat," he said with some emotion, "must be humoured,
not drove."

Here is another comically displaced emblem of the sexual
act. It is worth noting that the cabbage leaf contrasts with
Mrs. Gamp's in point of freshness. It is also worth noting
that an older and more experienced man is helping Tom
get the meat correctly into the pocket.

It is useful to remember that Tom is a good organist,
that it is his twilight playing upon the organ that attracts
Mary Graham to him, and that he is playing upon the
organ when she comes to him to tell him about Pecksniff's
infamous approaches to her. The scene takes place in a
church, naturally enough, and is clandestinely observed
by Pecksniff himself, just as the Dombey and Rokesmith
nuptials are also scenes in churches clandestinely observed from behind organs. We ought also to recall that
just before he is expelled from Pecksniff's house, the third
and last of the three son figures to be so expelled, Tom's
key to the organ-loft is taken away from him by Pecksniff
the pseudo-father.

Tom's relationship with Pecksniff is another form of
young Chuzzlewit's. They each leave Pecksniff's house
under conditions which suggest sexual rivalry with him.
In Tom's case that rivalry is more clearly revealed, and it
is Mary who is clearly the object of it. But Pecksniff is
not only the father. He is, as we have often seen fathers
be, also the progenitive phallus.

After Tom has left Pecksniff's house, his idealized view

of Pecksniff has been shattered, and this idea presents it-self to him through his perception that it is in the center of the Salisbury market-place that the statue of Pecksniff he had set up was gone. Tom's banishment from Peck-sniff's has in some measure meant his castration by the father. But the father is himself the phallus of which he is bereft. We are again at the level of unconscious ideation at which the father's phallus and the boy's are not dis-tinguished from one another. But when they are going out to get that steak, Ruth clearly restores Tom's phallus to him; that is to say, his and his father's at the same time. That is doubtless why, in part, the older and more experi-enced man is helping Tom ease the meat into the pocket with the proper humoring.

> [Ruth] . . . made the room as neat as herself—you must not suppose its shape was half as neat as hers though, or anything like it—and brushed Tom's old hat round and round and round again, until it was as sleek as Mr. Pecksniff.

Later on we shall consider hats in more detail, and the extent to which they can symbolize either the male or the female genitals. Mrs. Gamp's nightcap looks just like a cabbage. But here Tom's hat looks just like Pecksniff. It is interesting here to note further that Dickens amends his invitation to compare the room's shape to Ruth's with an attention-getting denial that there is any similarity or re-lationship. And it is clearly Ruth's brushing of Tom's poor pecker that renders it as sleek as Pecksniff.

One might analyse Ruth's steak-pudding making at great length, buttering the inside of the basin to make it nice and slippery in there, stuffing the basin full of meat, and finally pouring in a lot of water for gravy. But the point that is important, of course, is that Ruth Pinch's cir-

Ruth Prepares the Beefsteak Pudding for Her Brother Tom

cumambience is of interest mainly because she is the other half of the Loathly Hag in the novel. The exciting sexual imagery which attaches itself to Ruth's environment is expressive of her being the young version of the mother, just as Mrs. Gamp is the older version, umbrella and verbal diarrhea included. And Mrs. Gamp is of interest because it is she who rendered Silas Wegg in need of a prosthetic device. What is interesting to observe about the growth and development of the unconscious sexual mythology underlying the novels is that it is in the earlier ones that the mother castrates the father. In the later ones some sort of attempt at restitution seems to be going on.

In this chapter we have carried a good deal further the exposition and analysis of Dickens' props as they bear upon the unconscious sexual meanings in his fiction. The multitudinous host of props may be seen more clearly now to be a kind of hieroglyphic language. It is a language of images in which a small group of related sexual myths is being told and retold in a series of variations which repeat old meanings in order to express new ones.

We can begin to see that there is a mother figure who has taken the father's progenitive organ away from him. We have seen that the mother appears in two guises, as an old and unattractive, but powerful figure, and as a young and exceedingly desirable figure at whom one ordinarily cannot get. We have seen that there are frequently two father figures, or pseudo-fathers, and that there are signs of tension mounting between the two as the novels advance.

We have seen that there is conflict between the sons and the fathers, and that the sons have to fight their way upstairs in order to get at the treasures of the fathers. We have observed some of the sexual tension which mounts between some fathers and their daughters, and between some brothers and their sisters.

CHAPTER V

BEANSTALK COUNTRY

On Top of the Tallest Erection

IN THIS CHAPTER I shall conclude the explanation of those primarily sexual props we should recognize in order to appreciate the full implications of Bella Wilfer's wedding to John Rokesmith. It will also be helpful to the discussion of the intimate relationship between certain aspects of sex and certain aspects of death which is covered in the final chapter. Here the unconscious sexual mythology which invests the props with their meaning shall be made as explicit as can be. The emotional pitch of the sexual myths reaches one of its highest expressions at the Wilfer-Rokesmith nuptials.

It may be useful to remember that this book is about Dickens' props. Sigmund Freud's interpretation of dreams is used only when it helps shed light on the props. It illuminates them a great deal, but whenever there occurs any conflict between the two, it is the meaning which arises inductively from the props themselves which governs my choice of interpretation.

Once more I must mention the many meanings to which dreams and these novels lend themselves. The sexual meanings are not the only ones. Indeed, the meanings arrived at by an approach resembling psychoanalysis are not necesarily the most important ones.

Dreams tend to unite opposed meanings in a single object. The unconscious thinking which produces dreams is inclined to treat opposites as though they were an identity. The unconscious mode of thought is one which perceives no either/or. The meaning it expresses is *both*. Even the title *Our Mutual Friend* implies something of this nature. You and I are two different, and perhaps opposed beings. You and I, however, may be in some sense united by "our mutual friend." Even more than the more correct "our common friend," "our mutual friend" seems to bring us together in a single being. It is an important part of this novel, and an important part of the sexual mythology to which it supplies the capstone, that people, and meanings, which were separated in earlier novels, here appear united.

Jenny Wren, Mr. Venus, and Bella Wilfer provide new and unified incarnations of persons who have hitherto appeared separate and even in conflict. It is a novel which, coming at the end of a long series, brings to the surface that level of thought at which opposites appear as unities. It is also a novel in which those separated by tragedy and strife are reconciled. Certain types of people who in earlier novels were evil or antagonistic or rejected, are here redeemed.

It is a novel in which sexuality achieves the goal of rebirth. Again, there are a multiplicity of meanings not necessarily mutually exclusive. Rebirth provides the person reborn with an opportunity to start life anew. Rebirth, when it is accomplished with the aid of a new parent, can permit a new relationship with the new parent. One can, for instance, marry one's new mother. Jenny Wren, Lizzie Hexam, Mr. Venus, and Bella Wilfer all assist in the rebirth of important persons.

Dreams are an especially infantile feature of psychic life. This may partly account for their visual intensity and dramatically experienced quality, features which they have most in common with Dickens' fiction. It is natural that the wishes they bring to light should be among the earliest wishes one can have. These earliest wishes indeed pertain to that psychic state in the infant in which his sexual life is centered around the bodily functions and organs of ingestion and excretion.

Just as food is the most wonderful thing to receive, so feces are the most wonderful thing to produce, something of oneself, a thing of the greatest value, like gold. This becomes a symbol for it in dreams. We forget the extraordinary value which the child attaches to fecal matter because he is taught to regard it as a forbidden subject. Because of the way the infantile mind thinks, the early value he places on fecal matter is blotted out and forgotten. Fecal matter, because of its psychic value, is the first medium of exchange. It becomes the first gift one can give to the most important people in one's life, one's parents. Its value is moreover a sexual one because of one's feelings toward these important people to whom one gives it, and, furthermore, because of its place of origin. It is a long time before the child distinguishes the anal from the genital orifices. To him they are the same, and the sexual interest the child later learns to attach to the one is at the deepest psychic level related to the sexual interest of the other.

The force of much of Dickens' fiction derives from its expression of the deepest and earliest modes of thought. It is this expression of the child and of the child's impulses which most significantly contributes to the analogy between that fiction and dreams. It is possible to find the sexual and fecal meaning of money and other valuables repeatedly throughout Dickens' novels. It is, again, partly because that infantile level of sexuality is brought so near the surface that Bella's wedding to John Harmon acquires the visionary and dreamlike quality it has.

Tony Weller expresses infantile sexuality at either end of the alimentary canal. His propensity for mere ingestion, his powers of absorption, are matched only by the drama of his excretion. When he first produces that capacious pocketbook full of money and other valuables which he ultimately entrusts to the *other* father in the book, Mr. Pickwick, he does so in the following remarkable manner:

> "Where's the money?"
> "In the boot, Sammy, in the boot," replied Mr. Weller, composing his features. "Hold my hat, Sammy."
> Having divested himself of this encumbrance, Mr. Weller gave his body a sudden wrench to one side, and, by a dexterous twist, contrived to get his right hand into a most capacious pocket, from whence, after a great deal of panting and exertion, he extricated a pocketbook of the large octavo size, fastened by a huge leather strap.

The "most capacious pocket" into which he is reaching with such contortions for his collection of valuables sug-

gests the composite infantile pocket which indistinguish-
ably unites the genital and the anal orifices. So also the
"panting and exertion" accompany the act of defecation
here being symbolized.

The earliest primal scene in Dickens' novels occurs
when Oliver Twist, half asleep and half awake, observes
Fagin playing with the valuables from the box he took out
of the secret hole in the floor. In all the other novels the
copulation of the parents which Dickens sees as producing
the conception of the self are subsequent developments
and variations of this scene. This is furthermore an establishment of the identity at the deepest levels of unconscious thought between ideas of the sexual intercourse of
the parents and ideas of defecation or of buggery. It is of
further significance that in this early novel the form of
criminal activity to which Fagin attempts to introduce
Oliver is the picking of valuables out of pockets.

The sexual meaning which thus attaches itself to money
can be observed in many other connections throughout the
novels. It is apparent, for example, that it is the sexual
meaning of money which reinforces Grandfather Trent's
compulsion to gamble. He attempts to obtain something
for nothing, to seize the sexual good by a kind of rapine,
to render him a surrogate for Quilp's desire to rape Little
Nell.

It is not surprising that in the last novel of the series
the identity of sexual value, money, and fecal material
should come most nearly to the surface. The Harmon
fortune consists, after all, of enormous mountains of dust,
garbage, refuse, and, in short, human waste, feces. It is
clearly a gobbet of human waste that is unspeakably fished
from what is unequivocally a cloacal canal and introduced
to us in the first chapter of the book as the hero of it. He
is resurrected and does marry the pretty golden girl in the

golden bloom who, together with the golden money derived from the golden dust, constitutes the inheritance from his father.

Noddy Boffin is the "Golden Dustman." It is in the "midst of the golden bloom" that Bella manages to launch old Gruff and Glum "into blue water again." But like the other central symbols the fecal gold maintains its ambivalence, its expression of the two meanings, one of high sexual (and other) value, the other of waste, refuse, worthlessness, dirt. It is the latter form which constitutes the harbour "of everlasting mud" in which old Gruff and Glum was stuck when Bella came along and floated him. That is the form that appears in old Gruff and Glum (who is a clear representative, we must remember, of John Harmon's father, hateful old Harmon) before Bella's wedding.

> . . . most events acted on him simply as tobacco-stoppers, pressing down and condensing the quids within him. . . .

Among other things, the image is one of constipation. The value cannot be gotten *out*. John Harmon doesn't come into his inheritance from his father until the mounds have been sold and *moved*. For old father Harmon's surrogate old Gruff and Glum, Bella's watery advent acts as a releasing agent, rather like an enema, to get the fecal matter released so it can be transformed through something like birth into gold, into sexual value.

The tobacco-stoppers, furthermore, whether they are to be viewed as pressing down via the oral or the anal orifice, are operating symbolically in the manner of an unnatural application of the phallus to old Gruff and Glum. Until Bella is transformed by John Harmon his constipated old dad is being bebuggered. Bella's marriage to John Rokesmith transforms old Gruff and Glum (and John's hateful old father) from the role of being a phallus receiver to that of being a phallus projector.

The unity of diametrically opposed meaning expressed here in the small scene of the wedding exists also throughout the large scene of the whole novel. It is, after all, the same fecal matter which becomes transformed for Noddy Boffin and for John Harmon and Bella, with the help of Mr. Venus, into an inestimable good embracing both love and wealth. Silas Wegg, however, is covered by the fecal matter in the slopcart into which he is dumped. And Silas, one does not want to forget, is another major adumbration of the old hateful father, the unredeemable part, presumably.

It will help us in our quest for understanding of Silas Wegg to recall that just as he becomes a symbolic representative of old Mr. Harmon, the mean, depriving father, by moving into Harmon's old residence, "Harmony Jail," so also old Gruff and Glum symbolically represents Wegg (and old Mr. Harmon) at Bella's wedding to John Rokesmith. Both parents are present, in other words: Bella's father, and John's father.

Bella's mother is present as a wraith, and the pseudo-parents for both Bella and John, Mr. and Mrs. Boffin, are present hiding behind the organ (of course). The only parent apparently missing is John's mother. As we shall soon see, she is present, however, in Bella by virtue of Bella's bringing John Harmon back to life, a miracle she can accomplish because of her own transformation and re-birth. One good resurrection demands another. As we shall have an opportunity to see by the end of the next chapter, the events of the day of Bella's wedding are a revised and transformed version of an earlier symbolic scene. This was the occasion on which old Mr. Harmon saw spoiled Bella as a little girl with her father, Reginald, and decided she would have to be a part, a condition, of his son's inheritance. On her wedding morning when Bella and her father are preparing to go to Greenwich to meet John Rokesmith for the ceremony, Bella reminds her father of the occasion.

> Dear Pa, if you knew how much I think this morning of what you told me once, about the first time of our seeing Old Mr. Harmon, when I stamped and screamed and beat you with my detestable little bonnet! I feel as if I had been stamping and screaming and beating you with my hateful little bonnet, ever since I was born, darling!

It is worth remembering that at this point in the novel Bella has no idea that her husband-to-be, John Rokesmith, is John Harmon. It is further of interest to inquire into the nature of the bonnet, the "detestable," the "hateful" little bonnet. It is a part of the intense sexual imagery on the occasion of Bella's wedding that it is a bonnet which represents her vulva. Bella is beating it upon her father, who, as we have already seen, himself represent the progenitive phallus. And so she *feels* as if she has been beating it upon him ever since she was born, "darling!"

Hats in dreams or in Dickens' fiction can seem symbolically to represent either the male or the female genitals by a kind of displacement which is generally comic. In *Dombey and Son* Captain Cuttle escapes from his lodgings at Mrs. MacStinger's house to be caretaker of Uncle Sol Gills' establishment at the sign of the Little Wooden Midshipman. He is terribly afraid that his landlady, a widow with several children, a terrible temper, and quite evident designs upon eminently eligible bachelor Captain Cuttle,

will find him and recapture him. Mrs. MacStinger is a
castrating female much after Sarah Gamp's heart. The
language Dickens uses to describe Captain Cuttle's fear is
in specific terms of his being afraid of *bonnets*. The other
more alarming aspect of his fear is that Mrs. MacStinger
will take away from him his own hat (to add to a collection of umbrellas, perhaps), a hard, glazed one without
which he cannot undertake anything difficult, or, indeed,
even so much as go outdoors. A man must, after all, have
his manhood with him.

Sheriff's deputy Namby in *Pickwick,* exbeadle Bumble
in *Oliver Twist,* and Silas Wegg in *Our Mutual Friend* all
have their insolence rebuked by having their hats knocked
off their heads. In the early days of his acquaintance with
Sally Brass, Dick Swiveller only just barely resists attack-
ing her great brown headdress with the swordlike office
ruler in *The Old Curiosity Shop*. In a similar sort of situation of stress in *Nicholas Nickleby,* the Dotheboy's Hall
rebel leader puts on Mrs. Squeers' cap and beaver bonnet,
and takes from her the big wooden spoon, before he undertakes to administer punishment to her and to her children.

In *David Copperfield,* Aunt Betsey Trotwood threatens
Miss Murdstone that if she ever dares to ride a donkey on
her green again she'll knock her bonnet off and tread upon
it. Treading is, of course, a barnyard term of peculiar
appropriateness. Noddy Boffin crushes Mrs. Boffin's black
velvet hat and feathers when he kisses her in *Our Mutual
Friend*. In the *Old Curiosity Shop,* Mrs. Jarley, like Mrs.
Gamp, is another version of the castrating mother. She
doesn't have an umbrella, but she does have a willow wand
with which she invests Nell when she inducts her into the
ceremonies and liturgies of showing the waxwork figures.
She is therefore sufficiently powerful to protect Nell for a
time from Quilp's pursuit (a situation analogous to Aunt

Betsey's protecting David from Murdstone.) It is to the protection of Mrs. Jarley's bonnet that Nell retreats after seeing gargoyle Quilp materialize near the empty statue-niche in the gateway:

> The delight of the Nobility and Gentry and the patronised of Royalty had, by some process of self-abridgment known only to herself, got into her travelling bed, where she was snoring peacefully, while the large bonnet, carefully disposed upon the drum, was revealing its glories by the light of a dim lamp that swung from the roof.

Mrs. Jarley evidently shares with Quilp (and Nell), and with the cobbler in the Fleet, a displaced sort of family talent for sleeping in small beds.

But apart from hats and bonnets there is another well known sexual symbol on the head, and that is hair. When Bella gives her father his breakfast on her wedding morning she asks him:

> "What did I promise you should have, if you were good, upon a certain occasion?"
> "Upon my word I don't remember, Precious. Yes, I do, though. Wasn't it one of those beau-tiful tresses?" with his caressing hand upon her hair.

Ever since a considerably earlier period than the time of composition of "The Rape of the Lock," women's hair in Western European culture has been sexually suggestive. Dickens has his share of that sort of thing too. It is especially suggestive when it is let down and allowed to flow over someone. In *Our Mutual Friend,* again, Lizzie Hexam and Jenny Wren allow their long flowing hair, dark and golden, to mix and to flow over each other really quite voluptuously as they sit before the fire talking about Eugene Wrayburn.

In *Great Expectations* Miss Havisham plays sensually with Estella's hair. In a *Tale of Two Cities* Lucie Manette shelters her father with a curtain of her golden hair. In *Bleak House* Krook and Richard Carstone are both moved by the beauty of Ada Clare's hair, and, later on, so also is Esther Summerson. Aunt Betsey Trotwood touches Clara Copperfield's beautifully luxurious hair with great gentleness. That reveals that she is not, after all, altogether devoid of sensitivity to the same kind of "dolly" beauty which attracted her nephew.

In *Dombey and Son* "Good" Mrs. Brown almost cannot resist cutting off Florence Dombey's long hair, and it is Florence's long beautiful hair falling down that first moves Walter Gay to speechless admiration. Even Smike, dying in *Nicholas Nickleby,* cherishes a lock of Kate Nickleby's hair.

Dickens is nowhere more thoroughly and emphatically Victorian than in the significance which attaches to hair *color*. Generally speaking the men who are most desirable sexually appear adorned with abundant dark hair, while the women who are sexually most desirable are more likely to have light hair, hair that is most frequently, significantly enough, referred to as "golden" hair.

The contrast is most strongly marked among men, and can be seen especially clearly in the envy sandy-haired and whiskerless Fascination Fledgeby has in *Our Mutual Friend* for gorgeously dark haired and whiskered Alfred Lammle. Rumty Wilfer in that same novel, and Joe Gargery in *Great Expectations* are both light haired. While both men are lovable, and both certainly exhibit manly qualities in many ways, both are emphatically hen-pecked and wife-dominated. From the narrowly focussed point of view of sex in marriage neither is much of a man. Much as he pines for her, young John Chivery, who is light-haired, just can't get to first base when it comes to attracting Little Dorrit's love.

On the other hand, in *David Copperfield,* Mr. Murdstone's hair and whiskers (albeit shaved) are as thick and black as they could possibly be, and so, also, in *Drood,* are John Jasper's. In *Pickwick* Mr. Tupman's rival Mr. Jingle has black hair. Tony Weller's rival in the same novel, Mr. Stiggins, has long black hair. And again in the same book Tom Smart's rival for the hand of the lady innkeeper has long black wavy hair and whiskers. (That provides an interestingly rearranged parallel to the Weller's situation with Mr. Stiggins, for Mrs. Weller is also an innkeeper. In a number of novels there are highly desirable women inn-keepers or inn-owners. All the warmth and firelight and good things to eat and drink and all those beds somehow seem to provide a perfect setting for expressing all that is desirable in a woman. In addition, to be vulgarly practical about it, the value of an inn represents a significant dowery.)

With women the distinctions of color can less readily be drawn. Some of the most attractive women have dark hair or brown hair. Florence Dombey, Madeline Bray, Pet Meagles, Estella Havisham, Lizzie Hexam, Bella Wilfer, and Rosa Bud are among these. But the women whose hair seems to receive the most attention often have light, that is to say *golden* hair. Ada Clare and Lucie Manette are outstanding in this regard, and so, interestingly enough, is Jenny Wren. One thing is certain, and that is that hairlessness is unattractive. Numbers of mostly older women, like Mrs. Gamp, have their loathliness heightened by wearing

false hair. Even for men hairlessness is of significance. Mr.
Pancks revolts and symbolically castrates Patriarch Casby
in *Little Dorrit* by trimming his hat *and* his hair.

It is a part of Bella Wilfer's overtly flirtatious behavior
with her father in *Our Mutual Friend* that she waggles her
bare white foot at him. The significance of this sort of
thing can be more readily seen in connection with Jenny
Wren who most nearly expresses the same kinds of functions, relationships, problems, and even identities as Bella.
On the occasion when Riah accompanies Jenny Wren to
the Six Jolly Fellowship-Porters to clear Gaffer Hexam's
reputation, Riah comes through the fog from Pubsey and
Co. to Jenny's house:

> Miss Wren expected him. He could see her through the
> window by the light of her low fire—carefully banked up
> with damp cinders that it might last the longer and waste
> the less when she went out—sitting waiting for him in
> her bonnet. His tap at the glass roused her from the
> musing solitude in which she sat, and she came to open
> it; aiding her steps with a little crutch-stick.
> "Good evening, godmother!" said Miss Jenny Wren.
> The old man laughed, and gave her his arm to lean on.
> "Won't you come in and warm yourself, godmother?"
> asked Miss Jenny Wren.
> "Not if you are ready, Cinderella, my dear."
> "Well!" exclaimed Miss Wren, delighted. "Now you *are*
> a clever old boy!"

Like her author, Miss Wren, whose real name is Fanny
Cleaver, habitually thinks in terms of folk tales and folk
myth. This quality in her, indeed, like her having more
names than she needs, is not unlike the two duelling frogs
in Mr. Venus' shop window. She and Mr. Venus do indeed
express only sightly different aspects of the same identities.

Like her author, too, Miss Wren's command of folk lore is applied with literal exactness, at least insofar as some of the details are concerned. Riah does in fact find her sitting near the ashes by the fire after the manner of Cinderella. It is true that some of the other elements of the tale do not seem to apply to Jenny. There is no cruel stepmother, nor are there three cruel female siblings, nor a prince. A detail Dickens generally employs in other versions of this myth is not present here. That is, a magically identifying slipper which drops off at midnight and later goes back on with all the vulvic overtones shoes have in general, and all the personal connotations of shoeblacking that they have for Dickens.

It is true that Riah is associated with teaching Lizzie and Jenny to read and write, and that he is responsible for Jenny's rising up to the rooftop garden atop Pubsey and Company. We shall see the immense significance of these things, especially the latter, later on in this chapter. For the present it is enough to observe that an essential part of the psychic content of the Fairy Godmother's role in Cinderella is that she lifts Cinderella up out of her ordinary life into an immensely higher, socially and erotically higher, order of life.

Meanwhile, however, there is other sexual imagery surrounding Jenny we may note before passing on. When she and Riah leave her house together, she locks the front door.

But the key was an instrument of such gigantic proportions, that before they started, Riah proposed to carry it.

"No, no, no! I'll carry it myself," returned Miss Wren. "I'm awfully lopsided, you know, and stowed down in my pocket it'll trim the ship. To let you into a secret, godmother, I wear my pocket on my high side, o' purpose."

She has never really known what it was like to have a man in her life, and so from earliest childhood she has been a castrating woman, as her crutch and this key amply demonstrate. What is interesting about this novel, as we shall shortly see, is that before its end she is induced to give the stolen phallus up to its rightful wielder. It is another illustration of the sexual thematic statement made in Wegg's double recovery of the phallus of the father. It is a statement made most emphatically, of course, by the successful transformation of Bella's character. There is nothing, after all, more castrating than a mercenary woman who, in effect, brings the essential element of prostitution into the domestic circle.

Like cribbage, the sexual mythological significance of the Cinderella story first occurs in Dickens in connection with Dick Swiveller and the Marchioness. Dick literally takes the Marchioness from beside the kitchen fireside, away from the dirty, grubby chores. But unlike Jenny Wren, she exemplifies still further features of the Cinderella story.

While nursing Dick back to health, she tells him how she spied upon the Brasses. In this way she learned about their criminal conspiracy with Quilp against Kit Nubbles. When Dick learns about this, he sends her off to the office of Mr. Witherden, the Notary, to seek aid in rescuing Kit. The poor, slip-shod little servant keeps losing her shoes while she runs through the unfamiliar streets of London to the Notary's office where she has never been before just as Cinderella had never been to the royal palace. When she gets there she finally loses one of her shoes completely as she jumps, unnoticed, into Mr. Abel's chaise behind him.

In *Dombey and Son* the myth is repeated, quite explicitly this time. Florence is a poor little rich girl whose poverty is psychic rather than external. But at the time of the Cinderella episode Florence is in fact dressed as poorly as Cinderella in her original condition, or as the Marchioness, and is escaping from "good" Mrs. Brown. She hurries slip-shod through the unfamiliar streets of London seeking the office of her father, where she has never been before. On the way she meets Walter Gay, and, as she runs to him she loses one of her shoes. He picks it up and puts it on "the little foot as the Prince in the story might have fitted Cinderella's slipper on," but they keep coming off again and again, one or the other of them, and he keeps putting them on again. These shoes Walter later preserves in his own room. He takes them as a memento on his dangerous trip to the West Indies from which he returns transformed into a man and a hero. He then becomes Florence's Prince.

In *David Copperfield* Daniel Peggotty is the partner, a kind of alter ego, of Mrs. Gummidge's drowned husband. He protects and supports her, and she is deeply devoted to him. Here is what happens when he goes off on his quest for doubly lost Little Em'ly, his niece:

As to Mrs. Gummidge, if I were to endeavour to describe how she ran down the street by the side of the coach, seeing nothing but Mr. Peggotty on the roof, through the tears she tried to repress, and dashing herself against the people who were coming in the opposite direction, I should enter on a task of some difficulty. Therefore I had better leave her sitting on a baker's doorstep, out of breath, with no shape at all remaining in her bonnet, and one of her shoes off, lying on the pavement at a considerable distance.

Even without the instructive details of the bonnet and the shoe, and "dashing herself against the people who were coming in the opposite direction," it is easy to see here another highly displaced and refracted and comic fantasy of sexual intercourse.

We may note, too, that here is another coach like the one so heavily engaged in action in its "improper" chinks and crevices with Mrs. Gamp's fabulously phallic umbrella. She saw nothing "but Mr. Peggotty" on top, just as Mrs. Gamp was for five minutes face to face with the coachman, "go" wherever he might. Coaches do often seem to be like women's bodies, and the men who drive them, or even just ride of top of them, seem often to be performing progenitively. We have already seen that one of the earliest fathers, Tony Weller, in *Pickwick,* is, after all, a coachman.

One wants to remember in *Great Expectations* that the one rather fabulous set of lies Pip makes up about his playing at Miss Havisham's involves a remarkably elegant coach *which does not go.* It is in this novel that the myth of Cinderella undergoes still a further development and transformation into grim parody and reversal. In the suspended time in which Miss Havisham lives in perpetually unsatisfied "Satis House" she is forever half dressed for her wedding. She, too, has one shoe on and one shoe off. Her tragedy is that the Prince never came to put the foot in the shoe, or to make the coach go, to drive it. Here Estella is involved too. After Pip comes into his expectations, he is summoned to visit Miss Havisham again after a long absence. He finds sitting near her "an elegant lady whom I had never seen." It is Estella he has failed to recognize. She is holding in her hand the symbol of Miss Havisham's spurned virginity, "the white shoe, that had never been worn," and she looks at it. She laughs that castrating laugh she had learned so well from Miss Havisham.

Estella laughed, and looked at the shoe in her hand, and laughed again, and looked at me, and put the shoe down. She treated me as a boy still, but she lured me on.

As another emblem of her spurned sexuality Miss Havisham maintains a rotted bride-cake in the center of the table upon which the bridal feast would have been eaten. The frustrated bed and the frustrated board. She herself draws the symbolic relationship between her own body and the table by indicating that when she is dead that is where she will lie. She furthermore points out where all her greedy relatives are to sit when they come to feed upon her.

She is clearly a castrating mother in the form of a loathly hag of whom Estella is the attractive, albeit castrating, part. Her rank as a castrating mother, like Mrs. Gamp, or Mrs. Bagnet, or Mrs. Jarley, or Jenny Wren, is symbolized by the crutch she carries. But here the sexual myths we have been finding in Dickens' novels have undergone a curious development and distortion. Here it is not a father of the Bray, Barkis, or Barley type who is depriving the young man of the pretty girl, it is rather the loathly hag part of the mother herself, who is in this case the foster-mother, who is doing that. The man who would have been the depriving father, had he married Miss Havisham, was Compeyson. He has vitally injured Miss Havisham by never eating her virgin cake nor filling her virgin shoe. He has also gravely injured the real father, Magwitch. Eventually Magwitch get his revenge when he manages to kill Compeyson under water. One father kills the other.

As is true of many of Dickens' novels, especially the later ones, *Great Expectations* is almost completely lacking in real parents. It is strikingly rich, however, in its supply of surrogate parent figures with whom its various orphans can work out a whole panoply of parent-child relations, conflicts, stresses, and roles, far more, indeed, than would readily be possible in real life with real parents.

So also it is possible to observe here that the real father, Magwitch, is no longer the depriving father. He is not keeping the girl away from Pip. He doesn't even know she's alive, and if he did, doubtless he'd be delighted at the prospect of their making it a match. He is doing his best to give Pip all the money he can. It is the primary mother-surrogate figure, Miss Havisham, who has trained the girl to keep *herself* away and to be castrating herself. For a long time it is from Miss Havisham that Pip expects his expectations. Indeed it is from Miss Havisham that the only expectations come which in any permanent sense are conferred. They go right in Herbert's pocket and ultimately aid both Herbert and Pip.

The depriving, rejecting aspect of the Barkis-Barley-Bray father-figure becomes, in Magwitch's case, transformed into Pip's horrified rejection of *him* and of his money. This is a complete reversal which is added to Estella's rejection of Pip and of all men. It is only after Pip has had a change of heart and learned to love Magwitch as he is close to death that there begins to be the possibility that Estella may in time have a change of heart and learn to love Pip.

It is unnecessary here to go into all of the instances of symbollically phallic sticks of one sort or another which appear abundantly throughout the novels. But it is convenient for us here to refer to a foolish and frustrated young waiter at the Rokesmiths' nuptial dinner. He is

. . . an innocent young waiter of a slender form and with weakish legs, as yet unversed in the wiles of waiterhood, and but too evidently of a romantic temperament, and deeply (it were not too much to add hopelessly) in love with some young female not aware of his merit.

Weak legs are a dead giveaway. He is like young John Chivery, the weak-legged, who mooned hopelessly over Little Dorrit. John Chivery owns a walking stick with a hand on top of it which may, perhaps, remotely and indirectly be suggestive of masturbation. The only other person in the novels who has such a stick with a hand on top of it is Dick Swiveller. This stick appears after he has been abandoned by Sophy Cheggs, and before he has met the Marchioness with whom he plays cribbage.

In the *Old Curiosity Shop* before Dick turns to cribbage and gives up walking sticks with hands to their tops he has engaged lavishly in another activity which hints at masturbation.

That activity is flute playing, and a slight digression to consider this prop may be helpful here. There is a striking instance of flute playing in *David Copperfield* on the occasion of David's induction into Salem House where he has been banished from his mother's presence after he bit his stepfather, Murdstone. It is here that he forms two of his most important friendships, with Tommy Traddles and with James Steerforth. When David arrives by coach he is met by an undermaster, Mr. Mell, whose condition in life is scarcely more enviable than poor David's. That his condition is deeply miserable is made clear by his unfixable shoes.

"Here! [says the gatekeeper] The cobbler's been," he said, "since you've been out, Mr. Mell, and he says he can't mend 'em any more. He says there ain't a bit of the original boot left, and he wonders you expect it."

With these words he threw the boots towards Mr. Mell, who went back a few paces to pick them up. . . .

The truculent gatekeeper, Mr. Tungay, it is not surprising to learn, is "that cruel man with the wooden leg." He is a lieutenant, mouthpiece, interpreter, spy, and surrogate for the headmaster, Mr. Creakle, a quite phenomenally cruel man. Creakle is in turn a surrogate for stepfather Murdstone, a kind of horrific incarnation of all the terror and hateful envy the child David has invested in the idea of his father's gravestone. Mr. Creakle, like Murdstone and the older Mr. Harmon as well, is cruel to everyone in his family, has feuded with his son, and has expelled him from his presence, as did also Mr. Harmon.

"I am a determined character," said Mr. Creakle; "that's what I am. I do my duty; that's what I do. My flesh and blood"—he looked at Mrs. Creakle as he said this—"when it rises against me, is not my flesh and blood. I discard it. Has that fellow"—to the man with the wooden leg—"been here again?"

It is an interesting simultaneity of discarding, disowning "my own flesh and blood" especially "when it rises against me" and the wooden leg, displaced onto another person, of course, but a clear surrogate nevertheless.

In this siutation Mr. Mell is almost as abused and downtrodden as is David. For all that he carries out his orders to decorate David with a shame-conferring sign which says "Take care of him. He bites," there is a sympathy between the two, almost an identity of persons. On the occasion of his first meeting David at the coach to take him to Salem House, Mr. Mell stops by the way to visit his mother, and her fellow inmate, Mrs. Fibbitson, in the establishment for pauper women where they live. His mother is enamoured of her son's musical abilities and asks him to bring out his flute. Whereupon Mr. Mell

> . . . put his hand underneath the skirts of his coat, and brought out his flute in three pieces, which he screwed together, and began immediately to play.

The number three is in dreams a distinctive indicator of the male genitals. And this is a particularly appropriate location to keep them. What is outstanding about the performance is that it is so dismal.

> My impression is, after many years of consideration, that there never can have been anybody in the world who played worse. He made the most dismal sounds I have ever heard produced by any means, natural or artificial. I don't know what the tunes were—if there were such things in the performance at all, which I doubt—but the influence of the strain upon me was, first, to make me think of all my sorrows until I could hardly keep my tears back; then to take away my appetite; and lastly, to make me so sleepy that I couldn't keep my eyes open.

The activity is associated with all of the tragedy central to David's life. That involves his mother, his feelings about his mother, and Murdstone's disruption of their formerly happy world together. It also puts him to sleep, into one of those half-asleep, half-awake trances in which we have already observed Dick Swiveller and Oliver Twist observing such significant scenes.

> I dreamed, I thought, that once while he was blowing into this dismal flute, the old woman of the house, who had gone nearer and nearer to him in her ecstatic admira-

tion, leaned over the back of his chair and gave him an affectionate squeeze round the neck, which stopped his playing for a moment. I was in the middle state between sleeping and waking, either then or immediately afterwards; for, as he resumed—it was a real fact that he had stopped playing—I saw and heard the same old woman ask Mrs. Fibbitson if it wasn't delicious (meaning the flute), to which Mrs. Fibbitson replied, "Ay, ay! yes!" and nodded at the fire, to which, I am persuaded, she gave the credit of the whole performance.

When I seemed to have been dozing for a long while, the Master at Salem House unscrewed his flute into three pieces, put them up as before, and took me away.

We need not pause for a full analysis of this scene except to note that a father figure and a son figure both appear to be present (and both named David Copperfield after all). The flute as a phallic object is reduplicated by the neck and head attached to it which are squeezed. The sexual activity is identified, as we might expect it to be, with the fire.

There is tremendous guilt and shame in this situation. Later David betrays the circumstance to Steerforth who betrays it in turn to Creakle who fires Mell and expells him from Salem House. Ostensibly he does this because of the shame which attaches to a person whose mother is a recognized pauper. No one afflicted with such shame can be permitted to be a master at Salem House.

The expulsion, of course, repeats Creakle's earlier expulsion of his own son who had objected to his father's cruelty to everyone including his mother and sister. It is appropriate for Steerforth to be involved in the betrayal because Steerforth later betrays the much more important confidence David imposes upon him by introducing him to Little Em'ly. She was the first of the surrogates for his

*Dick Swiveller Plays the Flute While Thinking About Sophy Cheggs,
Little Nell, and the Marchioness*

mother, Clara Copperfield, with whom David fell in love. The scene and situation summarize the novel. Someone who stands for David is punished by a forbidding father figure for engaging, or for wishing to engage, in a displaced and refracted symbolic version of sexual intercourse with the mother.

Dick Swiveller's flute playing is not mother-oriented. It *is* Nell-oriented. It occurs significantly enough later on in the night after the first occasion on which Dick taught the Marchioness to play cribbage. He is very drunk on beer and purl and is cogitating about his three love-objects, so to speak. Prominent in these thoughts is Sophy Wackles, now Mrs. Cheggs, to whom Dick was all but betrothed until the plot to marry him off to Little Nell intervened. Dick's thoughts about Sophy, to whom he was evidently sexually very much attracted, are compounded with thoughts of Nell, who can be better characterized as playing a role of "expectations" in his thought, and on whose behalf he gave up the so-much-to-be-desired Miss Wackles. Into the midst of this amatory confusion thoughts of the Marchioness and cribbage come more and more intrusively replacing the images of both other girls.

Dick has, appropriately enough, gone to bed with one boot on and one boot off. At first the thoughts of playing cribbage with the Marchioness make him think of playing cribbage with Sophy. The trouble is, of course, that it is someone else who is playing with Sophy.

"These rubbers," said Mr. Swiveller, putting on his night-cap in exactly the same style as he wore his hat, "remind me of the matrimonial fireside. Cheggs' wife plays cribbage; all-fours likewise. She rings the changes on 'em now. From sport to sport they hurry her, to banish her regrets, and when they win a smile from her, they

think that she forgets—but she don't. By this time, I
should say," added Richard, getting his left cheek into
profile, and looking complacently at the reflection of a
very little scrap of whisker in the looking-glass; "by this
time, I should say, the iron has entered into her soul. It
serves her right!"

In this contemplation of the facial emblem of his
masculine powers Dick, in his perennial word play, is
doubtless thinking of *something* entering into her, and it
is something associated with cribbage or "all fours."

Some men in his blighted position would have taken to
drinking; but as Mr. Swiveller had taken to that before,
he only took, on receiving the news that Sophy Wackles
was lost to him forever, to playing the flute; thinking after
mature consideration that it was a good, sound, dismal
occupation, not only in unison with his own sad thoughts,
but calculated to awaken a fellow-feeling in the bosoms
of his neighbours.

There is no feeling of guilt present in this incident of the
flute, but there *is* a great deal of dismal depression.

The air was "Away with melancholy" a composition,
which, when it is played very slowly on the flute in bed,
with the further disadvantage of being performed by a
gentleman but imperfectly acquainted with the instrument,
who repeats one note a great many times before he can
find the next, has not a lively effect. Yet for half the
night, or more, Mr. Swiveller, lying sometimes on his back
with his eyes upon the ceiling, and sometimes half out of
bed to correct himself by the book, played this unhappy
tune over and over again; never leaving off, save for a
minute or two at a time to take breath and soliloquise
about the Marchioness, and then beginning again with

renewed vigour. It was not until he had quite exhausted
his several subjects of meditation, and had breathed into
the flute the whole sentiment of the purl down to its very
dregs, and had nearly maddened the people of the house,
and at both the next doors, and over the way,—that he
shut up the music-book, extinguished the candle, and
finding himself greatly lightened and relieved in his mind,
turned round and fell asleep.

It is a performance in which the loss of Sophy is relieved
by the advent of the Marchioness, the thought of whom
evidently enables Dick to continue playing his flute "with
renewed vigour." But he is about to abandon his walking
stick with the hand on the top, and that brings us back
to John Chivery and *his* hand-topped stick.

John Chivery is very much like the young waiter and
we have an opportunity to observe him in another scene
suggestive of masturbation. It is on the occasion when
Arthur Clennam has just been imprisoned for debt. Young
John, although he hates his rival, Clennam, nevertheless
chivalrously wishes to serve Amy Dorrit's interests faith-
fully. He rightly regards Clennam as one of the chief among
those interests, and puts himself out to take care of his rival.
He lodges him in the same room her father occupied in
the Marshalsea through so many long years. Young John
brings Arthur Clennam a light but choice collection of
delicacies for tea. Clennam scarcely touches anything, he
is so heartsick. They have been discussing Little Dorrit.
Young John cannot believe Clennam is really ignorant of
the fact that Amy Dorrit is wholeheartedly in love with
him. While they talk, young John finally reveals this truth
to him, so astounding to Clennam, so gallingly frustrating
to himself. While telling Clennam this, and torturing himself with the telling, young John

. . . fell to folding the cabbage-leaf that had contained the ham. When he had folded it into a number of layers, one over another, so that it was small in the palm of his hand, he began to flatten it between both his hands, and to eye Clennam attentively.

As they talk he continues "compressing his green packet with some force," and then "rolling his green packet on his right leg." Finally,

. . . Young John, having rolled his green packet pretty round, cut it carefully into three pieces, and laid it on a plate as if it were some particular delicacy.

Once again it is the number three which appears, as we have already seen, consistently to refer to the male genitals.

That nearly identical walking sticks which can be associated with masturbation should appear in the hands of John Chivery and Dick Swiveller suggests in the hieroglyphic language of the props that there are probably other and more important parallels of meaning in the sexual mythology in these two novels. Little Nell and Little Dorrit are similar figures in many ways, and their stories are similar. Both are involved in extraordinary relationships with their fathers, each of whom has a sort of remarkable financial problem, or, indeed, illness. Both achieve some sort of transferred or displaced sexual union with the father. Little Nell's occurs, as we have seen, through the agency of Dick Swiveller and the Marchioness. Little Dorrit's occurs because she marries Arthur Clennam after he has taken her father's place in the same prison cell. He has been served by her in the same way and even in the same clothing, and his figure has fused as much as it possibly can with that of Mr. Dorrit. The whole direction of evolution of the father-son conflict in the sexual mythology of Dickens' novels lies toward union of the father and the son in the same person. We shall be seeing more of this soon in *Our Mutual Friend*. But it happens here, too, in a measure.

Mr. Pickwick is the first to observe a foreshadowing of Little Nell and Little Dorrit, together, in the Fleet Prison, the prison to which *he* was sent for his indebtedness.

> On the opposite side of the room an old man was seated on a small wooden box, with his eyes riveted on the floor, and his face settled into an expression of the deepest and most hopeless despair. A young girl—his little granddaughter—was hanging about him; endeavouring, with a thousand childish devices, to engage his attention; but the old man neither saw nor heard her. The voice that had been music to him, and the eyes that had been light, fell coldly on his senses. His limbs were shaking with disease, and the palsy had fastened on his mind.

From the beginning Little Dorrit regards Arthur Clennam, "the grave, brown gentleman," as a father. "She thought what a good father he would be. How, with some such look, he would counsel and cherish his daughter." As we see here, and with Jenny Wren, the child has an inverted motherhood thrust upon her to care for the father who has failed to be a father to her.

The father-daughter relationship appears frequently in a prominent way in Dickens' novels. In *David Copperfield,* Agnes Wickfield is as close to her father as these other girls are to theirs, and broken alcoholic Mr. Wickfield is as dependent upon her as their fathers or grandfathers are upon them. She has been in love with David for as long a time unknown to him as Little Dorrit was in love with Arthur Clennam unknown to *him*. She is David's better self, as Little Nell is, in a sense, everyman's better self. David Copperfield frequently sees Agnes in his mind's eyes exhorting him to the good and the right and the upward path by pointing upward with her finger. This is a gesture which Dickens told Forster he visualized Mary Hogarth doing in *his* mind's eye. Dickens' own sense of identification with Mary Hogarth as his own better self, is fairly clear.

In *A Tale of Two Cities,* Lucie Manette is devoted to her father after his release from prison, crushed as he indeed is in his mind. She lets her glorious golden hair down to shield him. She nurses him back to health while he practices the manual craft of shoemaking, tap, tap, tapping on the shoe with his phallic hammer. Charles Darnay truly says to Dr. Manette: "I know that when she is clinging to you, the hands of baby, girl, and woman, all in one, are round your neck." And he adds:

I know that in loving you she sees and loves her mother at her own age, sees and loves you at my age, loves her mother broken-hearted, loves you through your dreadful trial and in your blessed restoration.

The various roles could not be more clearly or explicitly stated.

In *Our Mutual Friend,* the situation of the close father-daughter relationship occurs three times. We have already seen hints of Bella Wilfer's relationship with her father, and we shall see more. Lizzie Hexam's relationship with her father is an exceptionally close one, broken only by his death.

The third instance of this relationship is, of course, that of Jenny Wren and her father. Mr. Cleaver is dead and decaying before his time. He is a walking corpse, like Anthony Chuzzlewit's old friend Chuffey, and like dying Anthony himself his breath labored and rattled "like a blundering clock." Mr. Cleaver is so dependent upon his daughter that she cares for him as though she were his mother, he her child. She treats him just like a child, and gives no indication to anyone (except, perhaps, Sloppy much later on) that she knows he is really her father and not actually a child.

After Mr. Cleaver dies, Jenny Wren, like Little Dorrit, marries a father-surrogate, or at least we learn that she probably will do so, and we learn it in a very curious way. Toward the end of the novel Sloppy calls on Jenny to pick up a doll she has been making for Bella's baby daughter. They are meeting for the first time. Jenny declares she has heard of Sloppy's fame in "pitching somebody into a mud-cart," and Sloppy did punish Silas Wegg that way. Sloppy is so pleased that he laughs in his absurd way, like the goblin king, or Quilp, or Jasper, with his mouth so wide open Jenny makes the following comparison:

> "Why, you're like the giant," said Miss Wren, "when he came home in the land of Beanstalk, and wanted Jack for supper."

This is the giant who in the myth represents the father. Sloppy curiously represents a father-figure to father-starved Jenny Wren, just as Arthur Clennam represented such a figure to Little Dorrit. As we shall see in a moment, Sloppy is an interesting example of the coming together of the father and son figures.

Jenny conveys to Sloppy that the Giant, meaning himself, is ugly. And then she asks what he thinks of her appearance. In his embarrassment at the question Sloppy pauses, and as he does so, she shakes her head so that her hair inadvertantly falls down, her long, luxurious, golden hair.

"Oh!" cried Sloppy, in a burst of admiration. "What a lot, and what a colour!"

We know he is falling in love with her for the same reason and in the same way Walter Gay fell in love with Florence Dombey. And when in reply to Sloppy's question about whether she lives alone she says she lives "with my fairy godmother," we are reminded that she is Cinderella, like Florence, and that Sloppy will become her prince. The Prince and the Giant are fused.

When he looks at her impressive array of dolls, Sloppy remarks that she must have been taught sewing for a long time in order to do it so well. Jenny replies that she was never taught a stitch, but "just gobbled and gobbled" until she learned how. She has sewn a great deal, and produced many babies, that is dolls, by means of it. There are interesting suggestions here of notions of the magical ingestion of babies, and of anal birth. Sewing, like shoemaking, is a manual craft of a suggestive nature, inasmuch as it consists of a rhythmic in and out sort of motion. Among other things, Jenny is a Loathly Hag who is a little girl. She is a little girl loathly hag who happens also to be a golden girl. In the uniting of opposites which takes place in *Our Mutual Friend,* she unites both the attractive young and desirable part with the old, unattractive, mother part.

Sloppy has learned cabinet making, and offers to provide Jenny with certain props we already have encountered in Mrs. Gamp's bedroom.

"I could make you," said Sloppy, surveying the room,
"I could make you a handy set of nests to lay the dolls in.
Or I could make you a handy little set of drawers, to keep
your silks and threads and scraps in. Or I could turn you
a rare handle for that crutch-stick, if it belongs to him
you call your father."

Sloppy is terribly embarrassed to learn that the crutch-stick
belongs to Jenny, but with extraordinary diplomacy, as
well as with appropriate symbolism, he says:

I am very glad it's yours, because I'd rather ornament
it for you than for any one else.

She shows him how she uses it, "Hoppetty, Kicketty, Peg-
peg-peg." Just like a wooden leg pegging down a cribbage
board. "It seems to me that you hardly want it at all," said
Sloppy. He is telling her that at last she can stop being a
castrating female. The conflated father-son figure, Giant
and Prince, like Gabriel Varden is ready to cure her with
the cure that cured Martha Varden. She can return the
stick, properly ornamented, to him she calls her father, who
will turn out to be Giant-Prince Sloppy. And she does it.
    This is the novel in which the castrating women give
back the phalluses they've stolen to their men-folk who
ought to have and to wield them. Unlike all the other
earlier castration threatening women with their wands,
umbrellas, crutches, and other emblems of the father's
phallus, here at last is a woman who can freely consent
to give into Sloppy's hand the phallus torn from the father.
Sloppy has a mother/daughter with whom to unite; unlike
Silas Wegg he is able to accomplish the restoration of the
missing member. "And as concerning the nests and

drawers," said Sloppy, "why, it would be a real pleasure to me."

Finally Jenny asks what Sloppy has come for, and delivers the doll into his keeping, all wrapped in silver paper. "I'll take more care of her than if she was a gold image," said Sloppy. That is, at this level of unconscious ideation, more care of her than if she were by some miracle of anal birth a child born of the union of the Giant/Prince and the mother/daughter.

Jenny Wren and Bella Wilfer, as I have said, have a lot in common. It is not exactly true that what occurs in the one also occurs in the other, but it is nevertheless true that each sheds light on the other. Jenny Wren is, at any rate, a person of central importance in Dickens' unconscious sexual mythology. In some ways Jenny is even more important and more revealing, in terms of the sexual mythology if not necessarily in terms of the novel, than is Bella. She is both Quilp and Little Nell united in one person. What was altogether unthinkable in the earlier novel is here accomplished in the later one. The many ramifications of her meaning and power therefore greatly exceed those we saw in the discussion of cribbage. We have seen the way in which fathers and sons in conflict can be identified with each other. Sometimes they are identified with one another through a simultaneity of symbolic genitals. Sometimes, as in Martin Chuzzlewit, Paul Dombey, and David Copperfield, there is a simultaneity of names.

Jenny Wren represents a similar bringing together of opposites. At one level we are observing a kind of reconciliation, a bringing about of peace and harmony (hence Harmon) and redemption. At a deeper level it is simply an expression of the way in which unconscious ideation represents opposites through a unity. We have seen enough

already of Quilp to know that he and the goblin and Fagin
and Jasper all represent a part of Dickens, a part toward
which the complex gamut of feelings tended to be dominated by denial and rejection.

We have seen enough more recently of Little Nell and
the other daughters devoted to their fathers to know that
they, too, represent their author. The unity in Jenny Wren
is not surprising because both parts of it represent different
aspects of the complex personality of the author. What is
remarkable about her is that here the author has been able
to bring both parts of himself into something resembling
a harmonious expression in the same imaginatively realized
fictional being.

There is another kind of unity which is being brought
about successfully for the first time in *Our Mutual Friend*.
It has a bearing upon the significance and nature of both
Bella Wilfer and Jenny Wren, and relates them yet more
closely to each other. It has to do with a fact I mentioned
earlier: there are basically two kinds of heroines in Dickens' novels, the erotic and the caritative. The former are
the giddy, spoilt, usually golden haired sexual toys, or
dolls, who for the most part represent the attractive side
of the Loathly Hag. They represent the young, desirable
mother who is not, however, much good for any female
function other than that served in bed. The hero pursues
them with the greatest infatuation and almost always loses
them.

The caritative heroines are sexually attractive too, but
one doesn't immediately perceive that aspect of them because they are mostly seen taking care of other people,
fathers, brothers, and often the dollies who are more
erotically distinguished. The caritative heroines are usually
represented as daughters and sisters rather than as mother
figures, although they do make the best mothers. They

usually have dark hair. They make the best wives. It is the age old problem of man that he wants to have both Lilith and Eve. He wants one kind of woman to be his mistress and the other kind to be his wife. Ordinarily he is lucky if he gets one or the other. The ideal would be to have them both in the same woman, and that is Bella's secret, in one way, and Jenny's, in another, because each achieves something of that unity.

The paradigm for this triangle occurs in *David Copperfield*. Here the erotic heroine occurs three times: in Clara Copperfield, in Little Em'ly, and in Dora Spenlow. All three are giddy, spoilt dollies. David is infatuated in turn with all three of them. In turn all three of them are taken away from him: the first by Murdstone, the second by Steerforth, the third by death. In this novel the caritative heroine who ultimately becomes David's ideal wife is Agnes Wickfield. She is like a sister to him for a long time, and is a loyal and devoted daughter to her sick and decaying father.

This triangle occurs again and again in various combinations and permutations through the novels, especially those which succeed *David Copperfield*. Arthur Clennam is infatuated by young Flora and later by Pet Meagles, both spoilt little dolls. He loses them both. He ultimately marries Little Dorrit the loyal daughter who is loyal both to her own father and to the pseudo-father who later becomes her husband.

In the course of the development of the sexual mythology from one novel to another, especially in the later ones, Dickens tries repeatedly to bring these two kinds of girls together. In *A Tale of Two Cities* he makes the attempt by means of substitution. Lucie Manette is a giddy, spoilt, golden haired sexy doll. She is put, however, into the position of being a loyal daughter, a caritative heroine.

This is partly related to the substitutions of the two al-most identical-twin-like heroes, Sydney Carton and Charles Darnay, who are repeatedly put in one another's place in life and death. One of them gets Lucie, the other does not. The other sacrifices himself so the first can have Lucie. He enables him to have her, and so in a sense he participates in the having. On the way to his execution he receives a symbolic consolation prize in the form of a little seamstress, just like Little Dorrit, displaced in this novel by Lucie herself. The little seamstress meets him in prison, as a Little Dorrit-like character ought to do, holds his hand, recognizes who he is and what he is doing, and kisses him at the moment of death.

In *Our Mutual Friend* a further stage occurs in the transformation. Bella Wilfer begins as a giddy, spoiled, sexual toy kind of girl. Like Lucie Manette she is put into a close relationship with a dependent father who is nearly as much of a child as is Jenny Wren's father. He is, how-ever, as much nicer a person than Mr. Cleaver as Bella is a prettier girl than Jenny. But unlike Lucie Manette, Bella Wilfer is given an opportunity to reject the father. She also changes from the giddy spoiled kind of heroine into the caritative, caring kind that makes the best sort of wife. John Harmon really cashes in on his inheritance: not only does he get all the gold, he gets both kinds of girls in one, as well.

The father Bella rejects is not Reginald Wilfer, to be sure, but rather the substitute or pseudo-father, Noddy Boffin. The significance of his role is that he is the good, positive, affirming father who only pretends to be a bad one to enable both of his foster children, John Rokesmith and Bella Wilfer, to work out certain aggressive needs rela-tive to the father.

The relationship moreover makes John and Bella into

foster brother and sister. The situation helps to explain why Noddy Boffin's miserly play acting part is so difficult to credit, perhaps, at the level of the novel itself, but is so right and just and probable and appropriate at the deeper latent level of the novel's unconscious sexual meanings.

Bella, furthermore, is brought through a personality change which makes her the first heroine successfully to embody and unite both perfect mistress and ideal wife, both mother and sister-daughter, in one person. We shall see, therefore, that there is at a deep symbolic level sexual play going on at Bella's wedding which involves two kinds of fathers, both Reginald Wilfer himself, and old Gruff and Glum as well. This is why John Harmon, as we shall also see, is resurrected from the dead and is enabled to inherit all that gold matter—the dust, the money, the feces, the golden girl.

To underscore the solution to the problem of the two kinds of heroine, Dickens characteristically repeats it with variations in the same novel. Jenny Wren, just like Bella, unites both kinds of heroine in herself. If only in the matter of her hair, Jenny is the golden girl in *Our Mutual Friend*. She is also the final incarnation of Little Nell. We recall that when Little Nell and her grandfather first met Punch and Judy among the tombstones, she helped their masters, Codlin and Short, by sewing some of the clothes for the dolls. Jenny Wren is the dolls' dressmaker, the "little dressmaker for little people," and this fact is of the greatest importance in understanding her.

It is characteristic of the caritative, wifely, loyal daughter and sister types that they tend to care for the erotic spoiled dollies. So Agnes Wickfield helps nurse Dora through her terminal illness. So Little Dorrit tries to look after Pet (Minnie) Meagles Gowan in Italy. So Little

Nell and Jenny Wren, and especially Jenny, are seen taking care of dolls.

Aunt Betsey Trotwood had observed that David Copperfield, like his father of the same name, "was always running after wax dolls from his cradle." Dora is a pretty toy, a plaything, who treats David like a doll, too. They are, as Aunt Betsey says, like two pieces of pretty confection. Esther Summerson is a caritative type of loyal daughter who is put into a doll's house version of *Bleak House*. This is a relatively early and unsuccessful attempt to bring the two types of girls together. Lucie Manette, as we observed, is a golden-haired doll who is put in the position of caring for her father. Jenny Wren is a golden haired girl, with a father to care for, and one later on to marry, who takes care of all the dollies.

Jenny Wren also has a motherly role, like Bella and Lizzie. Considerations of death and birth, resurrection and rebirth, probably ought to be saved for the last chapter. But a part of the importance of Bella's transformation of personality consists in the fact that it enables John Harmon to come back from the dead. So Bella gives him life, indeed, gives him *birth*, from one point of view, and thus in some displaced sense represents his mother. He has furthermore fallen into water, through a trap door, and climbed out again, a situation widely symbolic in dreams, folklore and literature for birth. Much the same sort of thing happens to Eugene Wrayburn. He, however, is helped out of the water by Lizzie Hexam, and so she, too, appears to adumbrate his mother and enables him, like John Harmon, to achieve the ultimately desired sexual union with the mother.

We have already seen Jenny and Lizzie sensuously mixing their golden and dark hair before the fire while talking about Eugene. It is an expression of apparent female homosexuality which is relatively rare in the novels. Aside from Miss Wade, it is reduplicated only in the relationship of Esther Summerson and Ada Clare in *Bleak House*. That novel also contains a close pair of friends named Liz and Jenny, one of whom acts as a mother-surrogate for the central figure of the novel.

Jenny Wren's motherly role in *Our Mutual Friend* is something she shares with Lizzie Hexam. At an early stage in the novel she had mentioned to Eugene Wrayburn her visual and olfactory hallucinations of flowers and of children who are divinely bright who come to play with her and to lift her up. (Flowers *are* the sexual organs of plants, and the lifting up in dreams and unconscious fantasy is sometimes symbolic, whether the mind be that of a man or of a woman, of erection.)

When Eugene is hovering on the brink of death, and is, in fact, symbolically being reborn, he sends for Jenny so she can be with him. He wants her to smell those flowers and to see the children again and to be lifted up by them in the same room with him while he is so near to death. He wants her, in other words, to share some kind of sexual experience with him and Lizzie, who is there also. And she does. She lets down her long golden hair for him just as Lucie Manette let down hers for her father when he was psychologically in a condition not unlike Eugene's. And she sews in the room, just as Dr. Manette had made shoes.

Another aspect of Jenny Wren's large sexual significance is that when the children lift her up so she can smell the flowers, they lift her up to the Beanstalk country. When the phallus rises in an erection, the Beanstalk rises too, and there is naturally a garden full of flowers on top of it.

When Riah finally comes downstairs to answer Fascination Fledgeby's pulling of Pubsey and Co.'s "nose," he takes him upstairs onto the roof. And there are Lizzie and Jenny. Jenny clearly identifies the rooftop with her visions of children and flowers. She refers to being up on the rooftop as being dead, which is, to her, in some ways better than being alive, and exhorts Riah, when he conducts Fledgeby down again, to "Come up and be dead!" There are suggestions here, again, of the union of opposite ideas. "Coming" up at the top of a Beanstalk can, perhaps, adumbrate ejaculation. And the opposite of a life-giving ejaculation can be being dead. Orgasm reaches out into the infinite, before the beginning, before birth, and after the end, after death. It is associated with a different order of being. It is, in any case, Riah, whom Jenny, as Cinderella, makes her Fairy Godmother.

The beanstalk country and hence Jenny's sexual significance can be fully understood only by an appeal to Dickens' next novel, *Edwin Drood*. It is situated in Cloisterham, and much of that is beanstalk country. There are so many ancient church dignitaries buried here, there, and elsewhere, that "every ploughman in its outlying fields renders" to them "the attention which the Ogre in the storybook desired to render to his unbidden visitor, and grinds their bones to make his bread."

That Ogre, of course, is the gigantic father whom Jack climbs up the beanstalk to rob, and whom he finally kills, just as Jasper presumably desires to kill Edwin Drood. With the role inversion and reversal to which we have become accustomed in dreams, it is John Jasper who is "Jack." But as Deputy Winks indicates, Tartar, since he is a tar, a sailor, is a "Jack," too. And Tartar is Jasper's primary opponent and rival for Rosa Bud's hand, and, as we are about to see, Tartar is moreover a "Jack" who *lives* at the top of the Beanstalk. Like Sloppy, he combines the father and the son, the Giant and the Prince, the Ogre and the Jack.

The myth is an important one and is repeated through the novels. "Jack's" first appearance is at number 6, in the court, where Tim Linkinwater, you recall, told Nicholas Nickleby there were hyacinths blooming in old blacking-bottles.

> "And as to flowers, it's worth a run upstairs to smell my mignonette, or to see the double-wallflower in the back-attic window, at No. 6, in the court."

It is a garden on the roof, you perceive. And the flowers:

> "They belong to a sickly bedridden hump-backed boy, and seem to be the only pleasures, Mr. Nickleby, of his sad existence. How many years is it," said Tim pondering, "since I first noticed him, quite a little child, dragging himself about on a pair of tiny crutches?"

Later in his author's career this boy will become Tiny Tim, and later still, Jenny Wren. He has crutches, he is crippled and deformed, and he lives up in beanstalk country.

When Neville Landless is in exile in London he lives in Mr. Grewgious' building under conditions reminiscent of Alexandre Manette's incarceration. There he meets Tartar, who also lives up there. That gentleman identifies himself by means of his roof-top flowers.

> "I beg your pardon," he said, coming from the window with a frank and smiling air, and a prepossessing address; "the beans."
>
> Neville was quite at a loss.
>
> "Runners," said the visitor. "Scarlet. Next door at the back."

"O," returned Neville. "And the mignonette and wall-flower?"

"The same," said the visitor.

"Pray walk in."

It is Jack again, identified by the same flowers, and this time with the beans as well, living amidst his garden at the top of the beanstalk. But he is no longer injured or crippled. He has moved in up there and owns the place. Jack and the Giant have finally become one and the same person, as we saw beginning to happen with Sloppy.

To underscore the association, Jenny is there too outside Neville's window which looks out on the roof-top garden Tartar has established.

> Yet the sunlight shone in at the ugly garret-window, which had a pent-house to itself thrust out among the tiles; and on the cracked and smoke-blackened parapet beyond, some of the deluded sparrows of the place rheumatically hopped, like little feathered cripples who had left their crutches in their nests; and there was a play of living leaves at hand that changed the air, and made an imperfect sort of music in it that would have been melody in the country.

There is clearly a Wren among the sparrows.

We recall that Mr. Tartar was once instrumental in saving the Rev. Mr. Crisparkle from drowning. Tartar is, in fact, a "water-Giant." And Rosa Bud takes to Mr. Tartar immediately when she first meets him.

> Rosa wondered what the girls would say if they could see her crossing the wide street on the sailor's arm. And she fancied that the passers-by must think her very little and very helpless, contrasted with the strong figure that

could have caught her up and carried her out of danger, miles and miles without resting.

And just a moment later:

> This a little confused Rosebud, and may account for her never afterwards quite knowing how she ascended (with his help) to his garden in the air, and seemed to get into a marvelous country that came into sudden bloom like the country on the summit of the magic beanstalk. May it flourish forever!

Once there, Rosebud, herself a flower representing a genital, blushes in Tartar's garden. The help he gives her in ascending to his garden is the sexual act, and the flying or raising associated with the symbolic erection puts her up in the place where Tartar does, in fact, grow beans. It is naturally Jack's wish, now that he is united with and identified with the giant father, and hence owns the beanstalk premises, that the symbolic phallus may stay up and flourish forever. Especially so long as Rosebud visits its top.

There is one more thing to mention in connection with Jenny Wren. She was present when Paul Dombey the elder married Edith Skewton Granger. It is the pew-opener at the church who chases Jenny Wren, burdened with her father, away:

> Truly, Mrs. Miff has cause to pounce on an unlucky dwarf child, with a giant baby, who peeps in at the porch, and drive her forth with indignation!

But Jenny doesn't stay away. She comes back when the wedding is over and waits to see the bride come out.

The carriages are once more at the church door. Mr. Dombey, with his bride upon his arm, conducts her through the twenty families of little women who are on the steps, and every one of whom remembers the fashion and the colour of her every article of dress from that moment, and reproduces it on her doll, who is for ever being married.

And that is precisely the way Jenny goes about getting the latest styles to dress her dolls in.

It is really all right for Jenny to come to Dombey's wedding, for he returns the favor by putting in an appearance at Bella's. The party Dombey gives in honor of his son's christening is rendered in glacial imagery. The cold extends even to Mr. Dombey himself.

> He might have been hung up for sale at a Russian fair as a specimen of a frozen gentleman.

There is only one other person so described in Dickens' fifteen novels, and that is Mrs. Wilfer. The description occurs on the occasion of Bella's departure from the Golden Dustman's household because of his apparently miserly abuse of John Rokesmith. It is the act which signalizes her transformation into the ideal wife for John, and it is indeed the day on which they plight their troth.

> "I have left Mr. Boffin's house for good, Ma, and I have come home again."
> Mrs. Wilfer spake no word, but, having glared at her offspring for a minute or two in an awful silence, retired into her corner of state backward, and sat down: like a frozen article on sale in a Russian market.

And as we recall, Mr. Wilfer is haunted throughout Bella's wedding in the church at Greenwich by the wraith of his wife, who in some degree represents Mr. Dombey.

As I have already hinted, the three weddings, Bella's, Mr. Dombey's to Edith, and Florence Dombey's to Walter Gay, all represent one unified scene. There is a phallic cherub present at Dombey's and at Bella's. There is a wooden-legged man scoring at cribbage present at Florence's and at Bella's. Mr. Dombey is present to witness Bella's wedding, and Jenny Wren, representing Bella, is present at Mr. Dombey's. It is the church itself representing Bella's genitals which enables old Gruff and Glum to employ his miraculous erection in the proper manner, as the representative of John Harmon's father:

> When the shadow of the churchporch swallowed them up, victorious Gruff and Glum likewise presented himself to be swallowed up.

He's victorious because his son is actually obeying him by abiding by the terms of his Will. He's also triumphantly happy because his son has obeyed him in a disobedient kind of way which shows him love and shares love with him. Furthermore Bella gets old Gruff and Glum's theretofore chopped off penis up, and gets it in. During the ceremony he uses it. And when it is over he takes it out.

> Forasmuch, Gruff and Glum, as John and Bella have consented together in holy wedlock, you may (in short) consider it done, and withdraw your two wooden legs from this temple.

The wedding represents also the thing it permits. Again we have the familiar scene in which an act of sexual intercourse is being performed while at the same time it is being clandestinely watched. It is also a situation in which the father figure(s) enjoys a kind of displaced and symbolic "right of the senior" to the favors of the bride before handing her on to his son, her proper swain.

CHAPTER VI

THE DROWNED MAN'S LITTLE FINGER

How to Bring the Phallus Back From the Dead

"COME UP AND BE DEAD!" said Jenny Wren to Mr. Riah, her Fairy Godmother. It is an invitation which combines "coming," that is, orgasm, with death. We have already observed this characteristic of the unconscious ideation which produces dreams, and, it is my thesis, Dickens' novels. It tends to combine opposites as part of a single, whole unity. The positive statement of a thing often seems to have its negative opposite lurking about in the background, peeping over its shoulder, so to speak. This is true even when there seems to be little or no logical point to its being there.

In this concluding chapter I shall devote some attention to the ideas of death and dying. Sometimes violent death is an implicit and often inescapable part of the sexual mythology with which we are primarily concerned. Indeed, the positive, life creating aspects of the sexual meaning cannot be isolated from the death meaning without radically altering, perhaps destroying, their ultimate significance. One of the major themes which rises to a culmination in Dickens' novels especially in *Our Mutual Friend* is a theme of resurrection and rebirth. The statement of that theme clearly implies that there must be a death before that resurrection can occur.

It is evident that we shall have to accustom ourselves to dealing with contradictory materials of thought. Jenny's "Come up and be dead!" is, paradoxically, an invitation to a greater, better, more intense form of life. We must compare ordinary life with death. In some cases a person is more dead than alive. Life can be a form of imprisonment. Jenny's invitation to Riah is that she wants him up in her garden in the sky where he, her second father, can come. It is the country at the summit of the beanstalk where Jenny herself and Sloppy, and where Rosa Bud and Mr. Tartar, manage to unite the sexual act with death. It is up in the beanstalk country that Jack steals things of value from the Giant, and, finally, kills him.

Jenny Wren is on the rooftop of Pubsey and Co. in a state of death which is more lively than life. She shows us where it is that Little Nell goes when she is finally transformed. It is also where Little Dorrit goes to when she gets out of prison. Both Little Nell and Little Dorrit have within them a part of Agnes Wickfield and Mary Hogarth. They have within them that vision both David Copperfield and Charles Dickens see silently pointing upward summoning to the higher, better path. We must, however, never forget that Jenny also has within her that identity which sought to ravage the pure child. It is clear that one cannot get to the top of the beanstalk to find Nell or Jenny or Rosebud without having Quilp's dynamism within one, suitably transformed for the better, no doubt, but still there.

It is furthermore important to keep one's eye on the identity of the author. More than ever we must seek to trace him in his characters. It is clear that in his struggle to resolve basic psychic problems shared by all men, the artist Dickens was involved in the transformation of his own most intimate inner struggles and conflicts. It is particularly difficult to deal with ideas of one's own death. It is much easier to imagine someone else's death. Every man's death concerns me because it figures for me my own. The deaths of those characters who more intensely and deeply than others seem to embody the identity of their author are of particular interest. In them Dickens is most directly confronting the personal meaning of death for him himself.

We have already observed that Dickens seems to make a peculiarly heavy investment of himself in those characters who have many names, or none. Deputy Winks is one of those. In *Drood* he tells Datchery the Princess Puffer lives

"Up in London. Among the Jacks."
"The sailors?"
"I said so; Jacks; and Chaynermen; and hother knifers."

We have already observed that in some measure the Princess Puffer is a part of "Jack" Jasper's mind. Those Jacks, those sailors are evidently a murderous lot. Although they are all named "Jack" they are like Jasper in one way and like Tartar in another. But Winks' identity is quite uncertain. His other nickname is Deputy. He is not a real person but a representative, a "deputy" for a person. "I never means to plead to no name, mind yer." The identity of the author seems to be engaged more deeply in Deputy Winks than in some other characters. It is worth watching his roles and what he does. He is a gadfly and he is a spy. He knows people's secrets. And he watches what's going on.

Tigg's equerry in *Martin Chuzzlewit* also hides behind a camouflage of a cloud of names. He is called Bailey, Junior, to distinguish him from Old Bailey. He was also known as Young Brownrigg, Mr. Pitt, Barnwell, Uncle, and Uncle Ben, and his real name is presumably Benjamin. But his identity is really quite obscure. Jonas Chuzzlewit has to kill him before he can kill Tigg, the character in the book whose name and nature seem to be turned completely inside out by money. Somehow Ben seems to get resurrected back to life at the end of the novel. Elsewhere Young Bailey is referred to as a sphinx, and he is akin to the intimately oedipal group of characters like Quilp and Sally Brass and the Marchioness. Young Bailey moreover has a taste for older women. The one lady he "sparks" in the novel greatly to her titillation is Sarah Gamp, the archetypal mother-figure.

Probably the outstanding incognito individual is Mr. Nemo, alias Captain Hawdon, Esther Summerson's father, Honoria Dedlock's youthful lover in *Bleak House*. His only friend in later life was "Toughey," who is the almost equally identityless Jo. In a way Jo is an alter ego of Nemo's. He brings disfiguring disease from Nemo's grave to Nemo's daughter, Esther, so she is marked. Jo and

Nemo seem to be an example of a near identity between a man and a boy, a father figure and a son figure.

It is a part of the oedipal struggle portrayed in the myth of Jack and the Beanstalk as it appears in Dickens' novels that the son who kills the father is identified with the father who in turn wants to kill the son. It is another instance of the close relationship of opposites, indeed, the identity of opposites, in unconscious ideation. As we have seen, many of the fathers and sons are doubles of one another. In a curious way, Jack's killing of the Giant is an act of suicide. It is himself he is killing when he kills the father. David Copperfield is, for example, both his father and his father's murderer. On the one hand he pities his father's gravestone out there in the cold. On the other hand his *wish* is very much that the stone should *stay there*. The story of Lazarus risen from the dead frightens him very badly indeed as a child. This fright is renewed when Peggotty first announces to him that he has a father. That gravestone comes in out of the cold in the form of Murdstone.

What is the nature of the terror that Pip and Herbert Pocket feel as they sit downstairs under old Bill Barley? They perceive him as a growl in the beam, a giant's wooden leg boring in at them. It is the intra-uterine fear of the paternal phallus coming in at them. The feeling is akin to the terrors caused by the battered brass nozzle of Mrs. Gamp's umbrella with the circular patch poking out of improper chinks and crevices at the other coach passengers. It is more than just a fear, for there are those in the novels who are actually killed by such symbolic objects. One of the characteristics of Dickens' genius is that there is virtually never any imaginative possibility, no matter how bizarre or remote, that is not developed in specific, vivid, concrete detail.

Rigaud-Lagnier-Blandois is himself a phallic figure, his head the glans penis, as demons in cloaks and hoods often are. (And as is clearly also the case for Uriah Heep, whose head David Copperfield sees staring from the ends of the beams of the Wickfield house.) When he thinks he has put Jeremiah Flintwinch and Mrs. Clennam where he wants them in *Little Dorrit,* Rigaud is left by himself in Mrs. Clennam's bedroom. It is of the highest significance that in this crisis Mrs. Clennam's paralysis is momentarily abated and she has the free use of her *legs*. It is only temporary. Afterwards she goes into an even deeper form of imprisoning death in life. To her paralysis of motion is added one of expression.

This is furthermore the time in which Arthur's problems of conscience and the past are resolved. At this point Mrs. Clennam gives to Little Dorrit the power to produce for Arthur something like parental forgiveness and reconciliation. Consequently Arthur obtains release from the prison of the Marshalsea and union with his pseudo-daughter, Amy Dorrit. At this time we see the wicked villain alone.

> In the hour of his triumph his moustache went up and his nose came down, as he ogled a great beam over his head with particular satisfaction.

No one ever sees him alive again. When the House of Clennam collapses it executes him in its fall. It is a retributive act of murder and suicide in which the Clennam identity destroys itself and its enemies simultaneously. It is done in such a way as to indicate that its primary enemy is its own guilt. This is what Rigaud represents. It is a long time before they dig out his messy remains.

. . . it was night for the second time when they found the dirty heap of rubbish that had been the foreigner, before his head had been shivered to atoms, like so much glass, by the great beam that lay upon him, crushing him.

Fathers punish as well as beget. Here in some sense the two activities are united in one. This is one aspect of the simultaneity of orgasmic "coming" with death. It is the symbolic emblem of the gigantic progenitive phallus that has smashed him inside the house—inside the mother. Rigaud's death is the realization of what Pip and Herbert feared. If you are inside the uterus you have to watch out for that Giant's wooden leg coming in at you like an express train.

Rigaud's guilt is a generalized one. It is not clear which of his crimes leads to the crushing death. One of his predecessors, however, James Carker of *Dombey and Son,* also attacks a father-figure in several different ways. It is clear that only after he has taken the older man's young woman away from him that the father's phallus comes at him to smash him to pieces. It is then that he

saw the red eyes, bleared and dim, in the daylight, close upon him—was beaten down, caught up, and whirled away upon a jagged mill, that spun him round and round, and struck him limb from limb, and licked his stream of life up with its fiery heat, and cast his mutilated fragments in the air.

These horrible phallic executions are clearly nodes for a considerable variety of meanings. From the father's point of view the father is simply punishing the guilty son, and from the son's point of view, he is being punished for his guilty acts and desires. It is also the case that unconscious thoughts of killing can by the associative inversion of opposites signify thoughts of orgasm. The terror of the father's phallus coming at one like an express train can be a masked form of anxiety created by the repressed wish to be in the saddle, or, on the other hand, by repressed homosexual yearning. With the identification of the father and the son it can signify Jack's killing of the Giant. The son becomes the father, and, in this role, slays the real father whom he identifies as the son. The son's identification with the father's genitals can represent the deeply terrifying act of an incestuous orgasm with the mother, an act which, however, renders one godlike and confers immortality.

It is, in any event, always upon the head that the symbolic penis strikes. In *Great Expectations* it is Mrs. Joe Gargery's head that Dolge Orlick strikes with his phallic hammer. Just as Mrs. Gargery is very like Rosa Dartle, so this hammer to her head is like Steerforth's to Rosa's. It seems probable that it is the hammer with which Orlick strikes her. It is the hammer which ever afterward identifies him in her mind rather than Magwitch's old chain and manacle which he simply dropped on the floor as a piece of diversionary evidence. It is with a similar hammer that he threatens Pip's life later on. Mrs. Gargery makes inarticulate attempts, after Orlick's murderous attack on her, to convey to him that she is on good terms with him. It is a bizarre form of love making. Mrs. Joe, like other dominating, castrating females, secretly entertains the ambivalent desire to be dominated and forced to submit. Her husband, Joe Gargery, who shows in fair fight with Orlick how much more powerful he is than that murderous individual, is nevertheless passive to his wife. He is, God help him, too "nice" to her. While that enables her to satisfy her desire to dominate *him*, it frustrates her contradictory desire to *be* dominated by him. Dolge Orlick's nearly death-dealing, that is, symbolically orgasm-producing blow on her head with his symbolic penis has provided her a unique sexual satisfaction. Hence it is that afterward when she seeks to express her gratification to him, she refers to him by means of the sign of his hammer.

In *Martin Chuzzlewit* Jonas bashes Montague Tigg to death by battering his head with his cudgel. The murderous beating occurs in a somewhat ostentatiously dark wood, not unlike the one through which Dante gained access to the underworld. Such configurations of landscapes can be pubic.

It is further clear that hangings and decapitations provide injuries to the head or neck which can be emblematic of castration and which can equate life and sexual intercourse with death. We have already seen David Copperfield sleepily watch Mrs. Mell in ecstasy (the word she uses is "delicious") over her son's flute playing. She playfully squeezed the neck atop which the glans penislike head blows its flute so that he momentarily has to stop.

There are any number of hangings in Dickens' novels. Among the most interesting ones are the accidentally self-inflicted hangings of Bill Sikes in *Oliver Twist* and Gaffer Hexam in *Our Mutual Friend*. The latter is especially interesting because Gaffer hangs himself under water and thus converts himself into an object theretofore the source of his income, a corpse dragged under water behind the boat, an instance of his own "luck," in fact.

In *Edwin Drood* John Jasper's relationship with Deputy Winks is quite like Nemo's with Jo in *Bleak House,* except that it is completely unfriendly. Winks throws stones at Jasper's head and hat, and Jasper at one point appears to try to hang Winks by his own collar.

Some part of the oedipal conflict is clearly expressed in Smike's terrified prevision of his father's suicide in *Nicholas Nickleby*. He sees his father hanging from the hook attached to the beam in the attic. This is clearly only a slightly different version of the death-dealing beam. This experience of Smike's is repeated in *Great Expectations* in Pip's predictive vision of Miss Havisham hanging from a great phallic beam:

> It was in this place, and at this moment, that a strange thing happened to my fancy. I thought it strange then, and I thought it a stranger thing long afterwards. I turned my eyes—a little dimmed by looking up at the frosty light—towards a great wooden beam in a low nook of the building near me on my right hand, and I saw a figure hanging there by the neck.

She does not, of course, hang. She burns herself to death. The fire which burns her symbolizes the immense, long repressed sexual energy within her with which she has done lifelong battle. That fire rages out of control, consumes and destroys her. The burning is still another version of the beam-end hanging. It links the parental sexual guilt, both erotic and caritative. This has perverted and distorted Miss Havisham on the one hand as the primary mother-surrogate figure and Abel Magwitch on the other hand, as the primary father-surrogate figure. He is the actual father by blood of Miss Havisham's foster daughter. He is the financial father of Pip's expectations. He is a man under life-long sentence of hanging. He is a man who first greeted Pip by leaping up out of his parents' grave and making him see the world in a topsy-turvey fashion.

There are an interesting variety of real or imaginary beheadings. Bradley Headstone's frustrations are adumbrated by the way his "haggard head floated" around the Lightwood-Wrayburn quarters in *Our Mutual Friend*. Arthur Gride's head appears to Ralph Nickleby to be detached from its body after the plot to get Madeline Bray for him is frustrated by Nicholas. It is shortly after this that Uncle Ralph proceeds to hang himself from the attic beam.

As we think about symbolically significant hangings and beheadings, we see how they can relate orgasm and death to the identity of the author. In this connection it would be constructive to consider Aunt Betsey Trotwood's ward and lodger, Mr. Dick, because it is, after all, *Charles'* head that haunts him.

Among the apparently confusing but really very enlightening reticulations of David Copperfield's identity, one wants to remember that he is more than a reduplication or resurrected version of his father, David Copperfield. In his Aunt Betsey Trotwood's eyes he is a mistake, a usurper. Had he been born a girl, she would have named the girl Betsey Trotwood Copperfield and taken the infant away with her to rear after her own fashion. She would have rendered this female child as nearly as possible a reduplication of herself, Betsey Trotwood. She would have done with this girl, so real to her that she goes on a long time considering that David has a sister, very much what Miss Havisham does with Estella. And, of course, in addition to being Pip's node of erotic desire, his "star," Estella is, in more senses than one, also his sister. In a number of ways Aunt Betsey, who is really David's greataunt, fulfills for him the role of mother. She *was* present at his birth, and, of course, the most important woman present at a birth is the mother.

When Aunt Betsey was disappointed in the birth of David, she took into her home Mr. Richard Babley, better known as Mr. Dick. His entry into her life is coeval with David Copperfield's advent into life. We know that Mr. Dick, as a kind of surrogate for David's imaginary sister, is not involved in an erotic relationship with the mother figure, Aunt Betsey. Indeed, it is backgammon that they play, not cribbage. Aunt Betsey does, however, fulfill a caritative role for this socially incompetent, but personally amiable man. She takes care of him and shields him against the world.

Mr. Dick is a writer, and like his author, Charles Dickens in his autobiographical novel *David Copperfield,* he is trying to write a lengthy document about his troubles. Mr. Dick's Testimonial about his troubles is repeatedly marred by the intrusion into it of the decapitated head of King Charles the First. Thinking about the distance in time at which King Charles lost his head, Mr. Dick says to David

> . . . if it was so long ago, how could the people about him have made that mistake of putting some of the trouble out of *his* head, after it was taken off, into *mine?*

There is a part of Charles' identity in Dick, and there is a part of Dick's identity in Charles Dickens. In fact Charles Dick *is* Charles Dickens with the end cut off, which is just what happened to King Charles the First. He had his end cut off. And if you have a Dick the end of which, the glans penis of which is cut off, you can't really expect to play cribbage with it anymore, only backgammon. One may even add that like his author, the writer Mr. Dick is concerned about his mode of publication. He makes a kite out of his manuscript, and the only peace of mind he seems to know occurs when the manuscript kite, bearing Charles' head, is way up, up, up high.

"There's plenty of string," said Mr. Dick; "and when it flies high, it takes the facts a long way. That's my manner of diffusing 'em."

There is another Charles who gets his head cut off in Dickens' novels and that is Charles Darnay in *A Tale of Two Cities*. The only difference is that he has Sydney Carton stand in for him, or, rather, lie down for him.

The murmuring of many voices, the upturning of many faces, the pressing on of many footsteps in the outskirts of the crowd, so that it swells forward in a mass, like one great heave of water, all flashes away. Twenty-Three.

Here is a very curious circumstance indeed.

Of all of the aspects of the author's ego represented in the characters in his novels, it seems very clear that Charles Darnay and Sydney Carton are two (one, really, split up into two) unmistakable surrogates for the author. One is the worthy, but rather dull self. Even Charles Darnay's name is an echo of his author's. He is innocent of crime himself. But he is repeatedly brought to trial for crimes of which in *one* of the two cities, at least, his family (like Arthur Clennam's) *is* guilty. Dull but good Charles Darnay is rewarded by winning the golden girl who tries to be a devoted daughter and wife. The other self is unworthy but more interesting and talented. Sydney Carton is a drunken, gaming wastrel, but he has much more brains and imagination than Darnay. The two selves *look exactly alike*. The unworthy one *lies down in the place* of the worthy one so the worthy one can escape death and lie down with the golden girl whom they both love. Death in the guillotine and love in the marriage bed are here inextricably linked.

Every novelist, of course, imaginatively projects himself into more or less all of the characters he creates. Every creative artist of note exhibits the ability to transform his own most intimate joys and agonies into objects of general edification and amusement. It is certainly the case with Dickens, however, that some of his fictional characters more specifically incarnate himself than others, and some joys and agonies are more important than others. We see this in Smike's and Pip's prophetic visions of the hanged parent, in guilty Carker's being smashed by the train, in wicked Rigaud's head pulped by the avenging parent's gigantic progenitive wooden leg, in Mr. Dick's head troubled by Charles' head cut off, and not least in the Carton/Darnay identity of orgasm and beheading. Charles Dickens presents for the world to contemplate and wonder at his own most personal and deepest inner confrontation of the mysterious simultaneity of the head which batters its way out through the vulvic gate at birth, the glans penis which explodes in orgasmic joy as it batters in through the vulvic gate at conception, and the head which, for its sins, is smashed or cut off at death.

In Sydney Carton's death Dickens, who was deeply fascinated by strange coincidences, appears by some curious coincidence to have predicted his own death. Sydney Carton is one of fifty-two people who are all to be executed on the same day. The book makes explicit the analogy of the fifty-two people to the fifty-two weeks of the year. Sydney Carton, taking Charles Darnay's place, is the twenty-third week and that is the week in which June 9th falls. On June 9, 1865, Dickens was nearly killed in a train wreck, and five years later to the day, on June 9, 1870, he died of a stroke.

One of the paramount mysteries of death is what becomes of the identity. In turn this involves the mystery of what makes up the identity. For most practical purposes identity is determined by externals, the way a person looks, the clothes he wears, even when he is disguised. There are many people who disguise themselves so as to be mistaken for other people, even when the resemblance is not so great as it is with Carton and Darnay. We are all in some sense disguised behind the external aspects of our appearances.

Clothes often make the man, or woman, as is indeed the case in *Bleak House* with Lady Dedlock, as Jo testifies.

> Cos that there's the wale, the bonnet, and the gownd. It is her and it an't her. It an't her hand, nor yet her rings, nor yet her voice. But that there's the wale, the bonnet, and the gownd, and they're wore the same way wot she wore 'em, and it's her height wot she wos, and she giv me a sov'ring and hooked it.

Part of the secret of Honoria Dedlock, and of the way personality displacement occurs in Dickens, lies in the fact that she changed clothes with two people who represent different aspects of her guilty self. One of them is Mlle. Hortense who fulfills Lady Dedlock's *wish* to murder Tulkinghorn and who then further fulfills Lady Dedlock's conflicting wish to punish her guilty wish by doing everything she can to cast suspicion for the murder on her former mistress.

The other person with whom Honoria changes clothes is Jenny, the brickmaker's wife. She does this en route to death at the grave of the lover who in her youth gave her a child and eternal guilt. Honoria's vindictive sister, who had apparently loved Hawdon too, had told Honoria the child died. But in fact she lived. Her aunt reared Esther Summerson into a sense of terrible personal guilt because of her own shameful birth. When Esther is about to go away to school after her cruel stepmother's death, she ceremonially *buries the doll* with which she had identified and which had been her only confidante. Jenny, the brickmaker's wife, also has a child, but hers really does die. Esther helps bury Jenny's child and gives her own handkerchief to cover the infant corpse. That handkerchief Lady Dedlock later secretly obtains from Jenny. It is the only personal possession of her daughter she permits herself secretly to keep and cherish. Her daughter has become a wonderful and lovely young woman, but she embodies her mother's guilt. Her mother is, of course, the woman above all others whom Esther would love and cherish and pity and honor if she could. It is this handkerchief which Inspector Bucket finds, and which leads him, unravelling Honoria's guilty secrets, to seek out Esther to go in pursuit of Honoria fleeing from guilt toward death.

Lady Dedlock is able temporarily to elude their pursuit because she changes clothes with Jenny. (That handkerchief, significantly enough, is a reoccurrence of the one in *Oliver Twist* which Nancy took as a memento of innocence amidst the evil of her life. She took it from Rose Maylie and held it up as though it were a talisman against the murderous attack of her erstwhile lover, Bill Sikes. In *Oliver Twist,* of course, the central criminal activity is the stealing of handkerchiefs. Fagin makes his living out of stolen handkerchiefs, redolent of guilt and sin.)

When death occurs and the identity of the man departs, the clothing becomes merely a heap, except for exceptional beings like Mrs. Gamp. So after Drood's disappearance, when Grewgious betrays to Jasper the fact that Drood had no longer been betrothed to Rosa Bud, Jasper momentarily falls down in a faint as he realizes how unnecessary the crime was. His body vanishes, and Grewgious "saw nothing but a heap of torn and miry clothes upon the floor." After the beam crushes him in *Little Dorrit,* we have seen that Rigaud is nothing but a dirty heap of rubbish. In *Bleak House* Smallweed frequently disappears and becomes a "mere clothes-bag with a black skull-cap on the top of it." In the same novel, Krook, to whom Smallweed is related by marriage, appears to be at one point "a bundle of old clothes, with a spirituous heat smoldering in it."

In *Barnaby Rudge* Hangman Dennis who keeps the clothes of those he hangs, becomes himself a mere heap of second-hand (and second-hanged) clothes on the way to the gallows. In *Oliver Twist* Fagin's meditations upon hanging include the reflection:

> With what a rattling noise the drop went down; and how suddenly they changed, from strong and vigorous men to dangling heaps of clothes!

Sometimes the loathliness of the loathliest of the loathly hags derives in part from the fact that they are barely alive inside the heap of rags which constitutes their clothes, or even, finery. In *Little Dorrit,* one of the countesses at one of Merdle's dinners is somewhere amidst one of her dresses. The condition of Edith Skewton Granger's mother Cleopatra is much the same in *Dombey and Son,* and Lady Tippins in *Our Mutual Friend* is in much the same category. (Not *"much* worse than Lady Tippins," is the judgment Eugene Wrayburn expresses to Mortimer Lightwood after they have viewed the several-weeks-old corpse which purports to be John Harmon.) In *Bleak House* the proprietress of Jo's dwelling in Tom-All-Alone's is "a drunken face tied up in a black bundle, and flaring out of a heap of rags on the floor." We recall that Mrs. Fibbitson is such a bundle of clothes sitting in a large chair by the fire that David Copperfield almost sat on her.

Aside from clothing, there are a number of birds who also seem related to human identity. Jenny Wren may be the most important one. There is also Barnaby Rudge's Grip, who is nearly an anagrammatic reincarnation of Quilp. There is Mrs. Merdle's parrot in *Little Dorrit,* who bites his master's finger, and shows his heritage clearly by holding his head awry like Flintwinch, and by standing upside down like the goblins and Tom Scott. There are only two crows in Dickens' novels, both in *Bleak House.* One flies straight from Mr. Snagsby's shop to Mr. Tulkinghorn's house. It is he who gets shot by a woman who practised her marksmanship at Mr. George's shooting gallery. This is where the other crow appears. When Phil Squod at George's Gallery first sees Tulkinghorn's familiar, Grandfather Smallweed, "the apparition in the black velvet cap," he "stopped short with a gun in his hand, with much the air of a dead shot, intent on picking Mr. Smallweed off as an ugly old bird of the crow species."

There are some other props associated just with death. In *Martin Chuzzlewit* Jonas sleeps on a truckle bed in preparation for murdering Tigg. In *Our Mutual Friend* Bradley Headstone sleeps on Riderhood's truckle bed in preparation for murdering Eugene. It is the same truckle bed on which Betty Higden sleeps in preparation for death.

Light shining through drops of water is interestingly associated with death. In *Our Mutual Friend* Betty Higden's sentence of death seems near when her second attack of "the deadness" occurs. She watches a barge's towrope vibrating in and out of the water with the sunlight coming through the drops of water falling from the towrope like diamonds. In *Great Expectations* rays of red sunlight shine through the drops of April rain on the courtroom window while Abel Magwitch receives his sentence of death. In *Our Mutual Friend* the sun shines through the drops of water falling from Eugene Wrayburn's oars while Headstone delivers his sentence of death.

There are some curious associations clustering around Jenny Wren's father's death. For one thing his pockets are out:

> "Turn all your pockets inside out, and leave 'em so!" cried the person of the house.
>
> He obeyed. And if anything could have made him look more abject or more dismally ridiculous than before, it would have been his so displaying himself.

The thing that is interesting about this is that all of the bodies recovered from the river by Gaffer Hexam have their empty pockets turned inside out. The Gaffer picks them, to be sure, a circumstance which surely establishes his kinship with Fagin, were any needed. He never admits to picking them, however. "Whether it's the wash of the tide or no, I can't say," innocently remarks Gaffer. This is one of the several ways in which you know Mr. Cleaver is dead, or dying, on his feet.

Mr. Cleaver is actually killed by a passing vehicle when he is trying to cross the street while he is drunk. It is through the red, green, and blue bottles in the apothecary's window that the curious faces stare at his body. This scene, except for the colored bottles, was anticipated years earlier in *Pickwick:*

> the indefatigable perseverance with which people will flatten their noses against the front windows of a chemist's

shop, when a drunken man, who has been run over by a dog-cart in the street, is undergoing a surgical inspection in the back-parlour.

That Jenny's father, Mr. Cleaver, should resemble the drowned persons brings us back again to confront the identity of opposites which unites water and death with water and birth. Gaffer Hexam is a grisly kind of mid-wife who makes a living by taking bodies out of the river. There is no doubt that the bodies are very dead. Neverthe-less it is Lizzie's training in this occupation that gives her the skill and the strength to save Eugene. This act sym-bolically expresses her giving birth to him, a rebirth into a new life. The act of drowning gives access to death. The act of being saved from drowning is birth, that is, access to life. One has to drown before one can be reborn. One has to be reborn before one can change his character.

There are a number of people who die by drowning, whose final movements and positions are similar to those used in sexual intercourse which, of course, may lead to birth. In *Little Dorrit,* poor benighted Miss Wade is eroti-cally tortured beyond endurance by the petty pretty spoiled foolish mite. . . .

> loving her as much as ever, and often feeling as if, rather than suffer so, I could so hold her in my arms and plunge to the bottom of a river—where I would still hold her, after we were both dead.

When Madame Defarge and Miss Pross struggle in *A Tale of Two Cities,* no one drowns, but it is a struggle to the death:

> the two hands of Madame Defarge buffeted and tore her

face; but, Miss Pross, with her head down, held her round the waist, and clung to her with more than the hold of a drowning woman.

When one father figure kills the other in *Great Expectations,* the embrace is, again, voluptuous and the drowning is real. When we first find Magwitch struggling with Compeyson, Magwitch declares:

> If I had died at the bottom there . . . I'd have held to him with that grip, that you should have been safe to find him in my hold.

And at the end

> he told me in a whisper that they had gone down, fiercely locked in each other's arms, and that there had been a struggle under water, and that he had disengaged himself, struck out, and swam away.

It seems quite clear that Abel Magwitch simply did not want to affront Pip's sensibilities by saying bluntly he had held Arthur Compeyson under long enough to drown him. It was an entirely justified act of retribution enacted upon the wicked figure.

These passionate death embraces, which might as well be coital embraces, the opposite meaning, come to a sort of climax in *Our Mutual Friend:* "I'll hold you living, and I'll hold you dead," says Bradley Headstone to blackmailing Roger Riderhood. Later, when they recovered the bodies, they found that Riderhood's grip had been broken:

> but he was girdled still with Bradley's iron ring, and the rivets of the iron ring held tight.

Here again, as is usually the case with this prop, the images of prison manacles, irons and chains are looking, as it were, over the shoulder of the language of the text.

What is especially significant about this particular kind of drowning is that it occurs in the canal lock at Plashwater Weir. The locks we have already seen have mainly occurred in relation to coition. The aperture concerned does figure in birth. Here we are especially concerned with the identity of opposites, birth and death. Perhaps Riderhood and Headstone drown in amniotic fluid. The lock holds them like a womb, or like a grave. And unlike some of the other victims of drowning, or near drowning, in this novel, neither of this guilty, wicked pair is reborn.

Riderhood was, furthermore, himself the Lock. He was a turnkey, another kind of midwife, like Gaffer, and at the opening of the novel the Gaffer and the Rogue can still remember a time when they were partners. Roger Riderhood is a turnkey for the prison that is death. He admits Bradley Headstone and himself together to that place of incarceration, and they do not come out. He serves as the turnkey to admit Betty Higden to the prison, death, and she does not come out. He admits Eugene Wrayburn to that prison, and Wrayburn almost does not come out. While Eugene is imprisoned, there is a golden haired girl by his bedside, and there is a manual craft, not unlike shoemaking, emblematic of coition, going on in his presence.

These are conditions which attended Dr. Manette's long life-in-death imprisonment and ultimate release. There was the same golden hair and manual craft. We do not meet Manette's turnkey, but we do meet his son-in-law's turnkey, Roger Cly, who had been falsely buried and strangely resurrected, and who was so unwholesomely bloated, both in face and person, as to look like a man who had been drowned and filled with water.

But that could also be a description of the other turnkey we have been talking about, Roger (same first name) Riderhood, who was in fact drowned twice, once before he undertook the duties of a "lock," or watery turnkey.

There is this further difference between the two previously drowned Rogers. One appears in the novel which seeks to bring about resurrection though substitution; the other appears in the novel in which resurrection comes about by transformation. Lucie Manette is not transformed, but substituted. Charles Darnay emerges from his prison, and is released by the "Lock," the turnkey, Cly, only because his double substitutes himself for him. But his double, Sydney Carton, dies at the guillotine for Darnay so that he can, in some sense, also achieve a partial substitution for Darnay in Lucie's heart.

In *Our Mutual Friend,* however, the golden girl is not merely substituted for the loyal daughter and ideal wife. She is transformed into her and becomes the unified embodiment of both. So also no one takes Eugene Wrayburn's place. He, too, is transformed.

There are other important turnkeys related to birth and to death. The most important and the most central one occurs naturally in the novel in which prison is most important, *Little Dorrit.* It is old Bob, William Dorrit's favorite turnkey, the one who first dubs Dorrit the Father of the Marshalsea.

Time went on, and the turnkey began to fail. His chest swelled, and his legs got weak, and he was short of breath.

The well-worn wooden stool was "beyond him," he complained. He sat in an arm-chair with a cushion, and sometimes wheezed so, for minutes together, that he couldn't turn the key. When he was so overpowered by these fits, the debtor often turned it for him.

The Marshalsea never really leaves William Dorrit's mind and heart even during his period of wealth. When he begins to die, and suffers the mental collapse which accompanies his last illness, he calls, again, for Bob:

"I tell you, child," he said petulantly, "I can't be got up the narrow stairs without Bob. Ha. Send for Bob. Hum. Send for Bob—best of all the turnkeys—send for Bob!"

It is clear that Mr. Dorrit can't die without Bob, either. Earlier, in *Bleak House,* Mrs. Blinder, keeper of the Necket children's Lock is also short of breath. She keeps the Necket children locked in while their little girl mother surrogate, Charley Necket, runs outside their prison caring for them and supporting them. Her successor, Little Dorrit, does the same for her family.

Perhaps the most interesting of the turnkeys is Mr. Omer of Omer and Joram. He is interesting because he is explicitly an undertaker. He had buried all of the Copperfields, including David's father, mother, and half-brother. Mr. Omer is a turnkey who is exclusively related to the death rather than to the birth meaning of the lock. David visits him as a regular visitor to a prison *would* visit the turnkey on his way in and out. He visits him on his trips into Yarmouth for Barkis' death, for Steerforth's betrayal and Em'ly's elopement, and for Steerforth's and Ham's deaths. Mr. Omer, like Bob and Mrs. Blinder, is very short of breath. Like Bob he is dropsical. Like Roger

Cly or Roger Riderhood he is drowning in his own fluid.

It is at Yarmouth on the occasion of Mr. Barkis' death that Mr. Peggotty makes the basic statement about water and its relationship to birth and to death. He answers the question that young Paul Dombey asked about what the waves were saying.

> People can't die, along the coast . . . except when the tide's pretty nigh out. They can't be born, unless it's pretty nigh in—not properly born, till flood. He's a-going out with the tide. It's ebb at half-arter three, slack water half an hour. If he lives till it turns, he'll hold his own till past the flood, and go out with the next tide.

Mr. Barkis goes out with the tide.

There are any number of others who die under much the same circumstances. Death and water in this sort of association are pretty conventional, especially in the nineteenth century. They are not at all unique in Dickens' work. Louisa Bounderby, watching her mother die in *Hard Times,*

> Saw her lying with an awful lull upon her face, like one who was floating away upon some great water, all resistance over, content to be carried down the stream.

When Lucie Manette's little boy in *A Tale of Two Cities* sickens and dies, answering, no doubt, the call of the waves like little Paul Dombey, he is mourned over by the sighs of the winds that blow over his little garden-tomb, "like the breathing of a summer sea asleep upon a sandy shore." In *Drood* in the Cloisterham Cathedral the choir's and the organ's music rises like the sea, lashing the roof, surging among the arches, piercing the heights of the great tower, drowning the monotonous mutter like a dying voice. Again, in *A Tale of Two Cities,* in the passage when the two giants, Miss Pross and Mme. Defarge, meet to fight to the death, Miss Pross'

> basin fell to the ground broken, and the water flowed to the feet of Madame Defarge. By strange ways, and through much staining blood, those feet had come to meet that water.

And from the same novel we recall that Sydney Carton's last impressions before he is guillotined include

> the murmuring of many voices, the upturning of many faces, the pressing on of many footsteps in the outskirts of the crowd, so that it swells forward in a mass, like one great heave of water, all flashes away.

As we think about bodies being like bundles of clothes, and about pulling dead bodies out of rivers, we want to recall that Roger Riderhood fished an incriminating bundle of clothes out of the river to hold over Bradley Headstone's head. Mr. Nadgett also fishes a bundle of incriminating clothes out of the river which serves as evidence against Jonas Chuzzlewit. The evidence in each case pertains to an attempted murder, one which does and one which does not succeed.

Drowned bodies dragged under water behind boats evidently fascinated Dickens. He uses them more than once in the later novels. We have already had an opportunity to observe this in connection with Gaffer Hexam's mode of fishing as well as his mode of dying. In *Little Dorrit,* Arthur Clennam's worries and guilt make him feel as though a criminal should be chained in a stationary boat on a deep clear river, condemned, whatever countless leagues of water flowed past him, always to see the body of the fellow-creature he had drowned lying at the bottom, immovable, and unchangeable, except as the eddies made it broad or long, now expanding, now contracting its terrible lineaments. . . .

And again in the first chapter of *Our Mutual Friend:*

What he had in tow . . . a neophyte might have fancied that the ripples passing over it were dreadfully like faint changes of expression on a sightless face; but Gaffer was no neophyte and had no fancies.

There is also the manner in which Drummle's boat followed Pip and Startop on the river in a lurking fashion

like some uncomfortable amphibious creature . . . I always think of him as coming after us in the dark or by the back-water, when our own two boats were breaking the sunset or the moonlight in midstream.

In addition to going through a "Lock," Eugene Wrayburn's trip to death and resurrection is a trip down a river. So also Martin Chuzzlewit makes a long trip up a river to transformation in Eden. He undergoes an illness almost unto death and returns reborn to become a new and better person. Then too Pip's final transformation occurs on the trip down the river with Magwitch, in the course of which everything is lost. When their mission to enable Magwitch to escape to the continent has failed, and when Magwitch is in custody, Pip finally does the right thing for almost the first time in his life. He stays by the side of the dying

man who loves him. Even Little Nell takes a trip down
a river, but it is a one way trip; she doesn't return, like
Wrayburn, or Pip, or Chuzzlewit, and so she is not reborn,
she simply dies.

Passing though a narrow space into water can refer to
the intra-uterine life. Monks drops the proofs of Oliver's
identity (in a sense it is Oliver Twist himself) through a
trap-door into the river. And it is through such a trap
door that John Harmon was dropped when he almost
drowned.

One of the most interesting props connected with drowning appears in *Nicholas Nickleby*. It is the little finger of
a drowned man which Bulph, the pilot, has upon his
mantelshelf. Why a little finger, of all things? It is the kind
of specimen one would expect Mr. Venus, more properly,
to have. It is, after all, a modest phallic symbol, a little
pickled penis, and Venus should have it.

It seems clear that Mr. Venus, who is both the author
and a reincarnation of Messrs. Fagin, Quilp, and Krook,
had a hand, along with Bella, in the resurrection of John
Harmon. When Mr. Venus explains to Silas Wegg that his
heart has been broken by Pleasant Riderhood, Roger's
daughter, he says that he met her first on a foray down
to the riverside to pick up professional materials. He indicates that it was on the night that George Radfoot's body
was discovered in the river and identified as John Harmon.
He gestures toward a shelf and begins to say that up there
he has what he got that night. Then he changes his mind,
and doesn't tell Wegg about it. Later, when Wegg ques-
tions him, he says that his trip to the river that night was
simply for the purpose of picking up the body of an old
parrot.

Now a man in Venus' profession certainly knew all of
the ways in which one could acquire bones, legally and

illegally. It seems further clear that what he really has up on that shelf is not a parrot at all. He simply made up that story to fool Wegg, whom by then he knew to be the sort of man who would try to blackmail him if he knew the truth.

It's a good bet that on that shelf was George Radfoot's body, or at least his bones, pretending to be John Harmon in death as in life. Venus doubtless obtained it from one of his regular "resurrection men," who, like Jerry Cruncher, moonlighted by stealing fresh corpses for doctors, anatomists, and articulators of bones like Venus. Throughout *Our Mutual Friend* we have the opportunity to watch Mr. Venus' slow articulation of "the Frenchman," (who is, incidentally, in English slang, another "frog") and who is the skeleton Venus *says* he is putting together out of his supply of "human warious," the spare parts from the hospitals. From one of these odd lots he had obtained Wegg's leg. Because he illegally obtained Radfoot's body, masquerading as Harmon, he can't admit that he has it or that he has boiled the flesh off the bones. As the novel progresses, however, so also does "the Frenchman." After the Harmon-Wilfer nuptials, in which Bella so strikingly electrifies and resurrects old Gruff and Glum, "the Frenchman," according to Venus' testimony to Wegg, has been completed and sold.

We know better. Venus finished putting Harmon together at the same time Dickens did. Bella and Jenny Wren are complementary expressions of each other. Jenny moreover has Quilp and Fagin and Little Nell within her. When this compound person principally expressed in Bella has been able to bring John Harmon back from the dead, Mr. Venus, who is also the author, has *also* brought him back to life. This has all happened because of Bella's transformation into the perfect golden girl *and* perfect wife. George Radfoot's bones, pretending to be John Harmon's, can then come to life, just as old Gruff and Glum's do. Love, Venus and the author have resurrected "our mutual friend."

This brings us, finally, to our concluding consideration of the fourth chapter of the fourth part of *Our Mutual Friend* in which Dickens' sexual mythology is crowned, climaxed and fulfilled by Bella Wilfer's wedding to John Rokesmith. The chapter opens with Bella and her father rising early in order to leave the house surreptitiously without arousing the suspicions of Mrs. Wilfer or her younger daughter.

> Bella was up before four, but had no bonnet on. She was waiting at the foot of the stairs—was sitting on the bottom stair, in fact—to receive Pa when he came down. . . .

They have a hurried breakfast, or at least Reginald Wilfer does.

> . . . they went down to the kitchen on tiptoe; she stopping on every separate stair to put the tip of her forefinger on her rosy lips, and then lay it on his lips, according to her favourite petting way of kissing Pa.

That is overt and manifest coquettishness, and veiled, latent sexual play, down the rhythmic stairs, with fingers and lips, between the loyal daughter and her father. Bella has a present for him:

> "What did I promise you should have, if you were good, upon a certain occasion?"
> "Upon my word, I don't remember, Precious. Yes, I do, though. Wasn't it one of those beau-tiful tresses?" with his caressing hand upon her hair.

The unconscious meaning is pubic hair, and it is more sexual play between father and daughter. Bella has something on her mind that she wants to confess.

> Dear Pa, if you knew how much I think this morning of what you told me once, about the first time of our seeing old Mr. Harmon, when I stamped and screamed and beat you with my detestable little bonnet! I feel as if I had been stamping and screaming and beating you with my hateful little bonnet, ever since I was born, darling!

More sexual play. An aggressive girl, she has a fantasy of beating her vulva against the progenitive phallus which is her father. And there is someone watching. That someone is the other father, John Harmon's father, the negative, mean, depriving father. He will soon be watching again as old Gruff and Glum who represents him. Mr. Wilfer tells his daughter he didn't mind her beating him a bit, and anyway: "your bonnets . . . have always been nice bonnets, for they have always become you."

> "Did I hurt you much, poor little Pa?" asked Bella, laughing (notwithstanding her repentance), with fantastic pleasure in the picture, "when I beat you with my bonnet?"
> "No, my child. Wouldn't have hurt a fly!"
> "Aye, but I am afraid I shouldn't have beat you at all, unless I had meant to hurt you," said Bella. "Did I pinch your legs, Pa?"
> "Not much, my dear. . . ."

The pleasure is fantastic because it is incestuous. Leg pinching is the same sort of thing as beating with a bonnet. It didn't hurt his fly a bit. To facilitate their escape, Mr.

Wilfer leaves before Bella. She soon follows him and meets him.

> Behold Pa waiting for Bella behind a pump, at least three miles from the parental roof-tree.

It is a pump, again it is the symbolic three, and it is the parental "roof-tree," a species of beam. It is the fatherly phallus, here, perhaps, in its merely urinary guise. They take an early steamboat to Greenwich and there meet John Rokesmith.

> . . . Bella no sooner stepped ashore than she took Mr. John Rokesmith's arm, without evincing surprise, and the two walked away together with an ethereal air of happiness which, as it were, wafted up from the earth and drew after them a gruff and glum old pensioner to see it out. Two wooden legs had this gruff and glum old pensioner, and, a minute before Bella stepped out of the boat, and drew that confiding litle arm of hers through Rokesmith's, he had had no object in life but tobacco, and not enough of that. Stranded was Gruff and Glum in a harbour of everlasting mud, when all in an instant Bella floated him, and away he went.

We are apparently in a position, at last, to make peace with the negative, denying father. Old Gruff and Glum "wafted up from the earth" out of the "harbour of everlasting mud" is Murdstone or Magwitch, coming out of the grave. He is to be floated, that is, put into water, or given rebirth. He is the punished/castrated father whose progenitive organ is doubly and deservedly gone. Bella is the loyal daughter and hence the ideal wife. In this relationship she is symbolically engaging in a kind of sexual intercourse with her father, Reginald Wilfer.

The actual act, of course, occurs later on that day when John Harmon takes the role of her father and mounts her. But she is also the mother. She is both halves of the Loathly Hag, with the pretty half dominating. She is the pretty, ideal mistress, and the mother, just like Jenny Wren. She is John Harmon's *mother*. She gives him, resurrected, the incestuous thrill of union with her. But she has also resurrected his father, and, as we shall see, permits a union with him. This ideal being, this combination of Dora Spenlow and Agnes Wickfield for David Copperfield, as it were, symbolically engages with two fathers in an adumbrated sexual union: her own father, Reginald, because she is the supreme expression of the loyal daughter; John Harmon's father, because she is the supreme expression of the young aspect of the mother. And then too, we presume, John Harmon will himself enjoy her charms, because he is himself, and his father, and, in a sense, her father as well.

> . . . Gruff and Glum, stricken by so sudden an interest that he perked his neck and looked over the intervening people, as if he were trying to stand on tiptoe with his two wooden legs, took an observation of R. W.

He isn't flying yet, but he is getting elevated. He sees in R. W. (Reginald Wilfer) an animated bit of architectural embellishment.

> For Gruff and Glum, though most events acted on him simply as tobacco-stoppers, pressing down and condensing the quids within him, might be imagined to trace a family resemblance between the cherubs in the church architecture, and the cherub in the white waistcoat. Some resemblance of old Valentines, wherein a cherub, less appropriately attired for a proverbially uncertain climate, had been seen conducting lovers to the altar, might have been

fancied to inflame the ardour of his timber toes. Be it as it might, he gave his moorings the slip, and followed in chase.

Old Gruff and Glum is indirectly representative of old Mr. Harmon, so of course his quids, that is to say his symbolic gold and/or feces, cannot be released under the terms of the Will, until John marries Bella. That event operates upon him like a laxative, making the gold flow. Bella is his wife, come back from the dead, and so his timber toes are inflamed in their ardor. And his excitement, note well, in part arises because he observes the other father there too, in the form of a progenitive phallus.

The cherub went before, all beaming smiles; Bella and John Rokesmith followed; Gruff and Glum stuck to them like wax. For years the wings of his mind had gone to look after the legs of his body; but Bella had brought them back for him per steamer, and they were spread again.

The association is so close that both legs and wings are meant. The phallus is back, and, with the wings, it is up.

He was a slow sailor on a wind of happiness, but he took a cross cut for the rendezvous, and pegged away as if he were scoring furiously at cribbage. When the shadow of the church-porch swallowed them up, victorious Gruff and Glum likewise presented himself to be swallowed up.

His role as a parent-figure and also as a lover-figure is made quite clear, really, in terms of Dickens' sexual mythology, simply by the fact he's there in the church looking on. And like the frantic union of Quilp and Nell expressed in Jenny Wren and adumbrated in Dick Swiveller's games

of cribbage with the Marchioness, Gruff and Glum here
is the second of the two fathers. He comes after Reginald,
but before the husband, John Harmon, to claim the "right
of the senior," and to enjoy Bella's symbolic sexual orifice,
represented by the church and its porch.

> And by this time the cherubic parent was so fearful of
> surprise, that, but for the two wooden legs on which
> Gruff and Glum was reassuringly mounted, his conscience
> might have introduced, in the person of that pensioner,
> his own stately lady disguised, arrived at Greenwich in a
> car and griffins, like the spiteful Fairy at the christenings
> of the Princesses, to do something dreadful to the mar-
> riage service. And truly, he had a momentary reason to
> be pale of face, and to whisper to Bella, "You don't
> think that can be your Ma; do you, my dear?" on ac-
> count of a mysterious rustling and a stealthy movement
> somewhere in the remote neighborhood of the organ,
> though it was gone directly and was heard no more. Al-
> beit it was heard of afterwards, as will afterwards be read
> in this veracious register of marriage.

Present are Nicodemus Boffin and his lady, who are looking for the orphan (that is, the author's identity). They
act as foster parents to both Bella and John. They are
there because they have played such a major role in making the marriage possible. And at last we can see the extent to which these clandestinely watched scenes in
churches are "primal scenes." The parents are there, including both forms of the father, both the affirming and
the denying. The observers are hidden near the organ.
The enabling of the act is, symbolically, the act itself.

> Who taketh? I, John, and so do I, Bella. Who giveth?
> I, R. W. Forasmuch, Gruff and Glum, as John and Bella

have consented together in holy wedlock, you may (in short) consider it done, and withdraw your two wooden legs from this temple. To the foregoing purport, the Minister speaking, as directed by the Rubric, to the People, selectly represented in the present instance by G. and G. above mentioned.

This is, again, the second father enjoying the sexual rights of the bride, his wife, the groom's mother.

And now, the church-porch having swallowed up Bella Wilfer for ever and ever, had it not in its power to relinquish that young woman, but slid into the happy sunlight, Mrs. John Rokesmith instead. And long on the bright steps stood Gruff and Glum, looking after the pretty bride, with a narcotic consciousness of having dreamed a dream.

Like all other son/father figures attending "primal scenes," he's half asleep and half awake having a dream within a dream. It is the anal birth image again. The child was ingested, and is reborn anew. The bridal party thereupon repair to "Mr. and Mrs. John Rokesmith's cottage on Blackheath, where breakfast was ready." There they are met by "a fluttering young damsel, all pink and ribbons. . . ."

This same young damsel was Bella's servingmaid, and unto her did deliver a bunch of keys, commanding treasures in the way of drysaltery, groceries, jams and pickles, the investigation of which made pastime after breakfast, when Bella declared that "Pa must taste everything, John dear, or it will never be lucky," and when Pa had all sorts of things poked into his mouth, and didn't quite know what to do with them when they were put there.

With the usual transference and displacement it is clear, at any rate, that *something* will be put into *somewhere,* and that the virginal somewhere will be unaccustomed to the experience. The whole scene is so sexually exciting there is a great superfluity of phalluses. The keys, naturally, are on her wedding day delivered into Bella's hand.

> Then they, all three, went out for a charming ride, and for a charming stroll among heath and bloom, and there behold the identical Gruff and Glum with his wooden legs horizontally disposed before him, apparently sitting meditating on the vicissitudes of life! To whom said Bella, in her lighthearted surprise: "Oh! How are you again? What a dear old pensioner you are!" To which Gruff and Glum responded that he see her married this morning my Beauty, and that if it warn't a liberty he wished her ji and the fairest of fair wind and weather; further, in a general way requesting to know what cheer? and scrambling upon his two wooden legs to salute, hat in hand, ship-shape, with the gallantry of a man-of-war's-man and a heart of oak.

All three of them, that is, the emblem of the male genital, did indeed have a charming ride on Bella that wedding day after all of the unaccustomed phallic things were put into the place that didn't know quite what to do with them. And old Mr. Harmon, with his hat, that is, his phallus in his hand, is reborn, or launched anew into the water.

> It was a pleasant sight, in the midst of the golden bloom, to see this salt old Gruff and Glum waving his shovel hat at Bella, while his thin white hair flowed free, as if she had once more launched him into blue water again.

The bloom in which he waves his phallus at Bella is golden because of the great sexual value which attaches to the golden feces she has released in him for his son, and of course, for himself. Then there is some more sexual play designed to identify John Harmon with the father:

> "You know that you have only made a new relation who will be as fond of you and as thankful to you—for my sake and your own sake both—as I am; don't you, dear little Pa? Look here, Pa!" Bella put her finger on her own lip, and then on Pa's, then on her own lip again, and then on her husband's. "Now we are a partnership of three, dear Pa."

It is the same three again. The father and the son are identified in the same set of progenitive genitals and are availing themselves of the same set of lips. And Jack is there at the dinner, too, naturally. He appears in the form of a headwaiter:

> . . . a solemn gentleman in black clothes and a white cravat, who looked much more like a clergyman than *the* clergyman, and seemed to have mounted a great deal in the church: not to say, scaled the steeple.

And just as Little Dorrit had her John Chivery, so also

> there was an innocent young waiter of a slender form and with weakish legs, as yet unversed in the wiles of waiterhood, and but too evidently of a romantic temperament, and deeply (it were not too much to add hopelessly) in love with some young female not aware of his merit.

He attracts the Headwaiter's ire by mooning over Bella and through another symbolic act.

> He finding, by ill-fortune, a piece of orange-flower somewhere in the lobbies, now approached undetected with the same in a finger-glass, and placed it on Bella's right hand.

At last it is time for Mr. Wilfer to leave.

> The amiable cherub embraced his daughter, and took his flight to the steamboat which was to convey him to London, and was then lying at the floating pier, doing its best to bump the same to bits.

Another emblem of sexual intercourse. But before the boat sails Mr. Wilfer has one more farewell conversation with his daughter.

> "Pa, dear!" cried Bella, beckoning him with her parasol to approach the side, and bending gracefully to whisper.

She is both halves of the Loathly Hag, and so she is naturally in possession of a parasol.

> "Yes, my darling."
> "Did I beat you much with that horrid little bonnet, Pa?"
> "Nothing to speak of, my dear."
> "Did I pinch your legs, Pa?"
> "Only nicely, my pet."
> "You are sure you quite forgive me, Pa? Please, Pa, please forgive me quite!"

The scene and the chapter end with another reminder of the early scene at which old Mr. Harmon observed the spoiled little sexy doll beating her father with her bonnet, and pinching his legs. His decision to saddle his son with her is fulfilled at Bella's wedding, after her transformation, to resurrected John Harmon. It is a combination of the primal scene of the sexual intercourse of the parents with the incestuous scene of the father's copulation with the daughter, and the son's copulation with the mother. It enables John Harmon, in some displaced and refracted sense, to be in his father's place in the act of his own begetting. He and his father are, at that moment, one. It renders him, therefore, in some remote but definite sense divine.

AFTERWORD

It is a chastening thought to me that Charles Dickens himself might have viewed the foregoing with horror and outrage. It does, after all, continually needle away at what must have been a number of very sore spots in his psyche. I personally find it quite depressing to contemplate the fact that he almost certainly would have regarded what I have written about him as being in the worst possible taste.

The depression comes, I suppose, from the interesting fact that one feels personally loyal to Charles Dickens, a kind of feeling which in general is useless for the production of a learned book. From a certain point of view, I suppose, the six chapters just concluded rather strikingly ignore the fact of Charles Dickens' greatness as a creative artist. If it does not altogether treat Charles Dickens as a kind of clinical case, this book certainly does, in its single-minded concern with the language of the props and the mythology of unconscious sexual meaning which they reveal, have little or nothing to do with the purely artistic aspects of Dickens' creations.

The uncovering of the most deeply felt concerns of

Dickens' psychic life, and their obviously intimate effect on the very core of his creative work, has everything to do with his greatness as an artist, however. It means he was concerned. It makes Dickens, heaven help us, relevant.

Charles Dickens was apparently engaged all his life in a profound psychic struggle within and among the various elements of his powerful, complex, extraordinary personality. It was a struggle which tore him apart, probably played a large part in ruining his marriage, and drove him through a variety of almost compulsive activities. In the end, it took such a toll on his physical and psychic energy, immense as that energy was, that it killed him.

This inner struggle, much of which could only have been remotely and indirectly present in Dickens' conscious mind, was very largely present in his artistic endeavors. The ideas, the desires, the interests Dickens struggled with for himself, he also struggled with on behalf of the rest of mankind. A great deal of Dickens' popularity, and a great deal of the enormous power of his fiction must derive from the fact that he confronted his own inner struggle in such basic terms as to make it everyman's struggle. It was an heroic inner conflict which appears hidden under the surface of his novels.

Even when the reader is not consciously aware of the meanings hidden underneath the surface of Dickens' fiction, he senses what is going on. He is able to do this, in part at least, because of the language of the props. It is a language which derives its force partly from the universality of the symbols it employs, and partly from the powerful trains of association which it builds and with which it then works.

Even when the manifest content of the novels is contrived or sentimental or artificial, the latent content of the deeper level of meaning is communicated to the reader.

This renders the more superficial imperfections unimportant. And because one senses this inner meaning, and recognizes that in some way Dickens is engaged in an heroic and monumental struggle for us all, one feels a great sense of personal affection and loyality for the man, even a century later, and even through the improbable medium of a learned book.

APPENDIX

The Old Curiosity Shop

THIRTEEN YEAR OLD Ellen Trent, better known as Little Nell, is an orphan who lives with her grandfather in his antique shop, the *Old Curiosity Shop*. Little Nell and her grandfather are completely devoted to each other. Indeed, his fondest wish and ruling passion is to leave her rich. His means for achieving this end is unfortunate, for Grandfather Trent is afflicted with a gambling mania. It takes the form of a belief that Nell is so good and so pure, and so beautiful, that Providence will surely reward with success any wager on the cards made in her behalf. The odds, of course, do not take account of Little Nell's goodness, beauty and purity, and her grandfather's secret gambling is in fact bringing them swiftly to financial ruin. The modest household is served by Christopher Nubbles, a boy about Nell's age who is utterly devoted to her interests.

Nell's wastrel brother Frederick in interested only in whatever money he thinks he can, through her influence, get out of the old man. Fred and his equally dissipated friend, Richard Swiveller, have, in fact, concocted a scheme to promote Dick's suit for Little Nell's hand in marriage. Their object is to obtain all of the Trent money which Nell's devoted grandfather will undoubtedly leave her.

The older Mr. Trent's clandestine nightly gambling becomes more and more desperate. As his losses mount, he becomes deeply indebted to a vicious, unprincipled moneylender, the crippled dwarf Daniel Quilp. Soon Quilp discovers the secret of Mr. Trent's demented gambling and seizes the Old Curiosity Shop together with all of the Trent property as security. Old Mr. Trent falls into a raging fever. He recovers slowly and thereafter is much enfeebled in mind and body. For the time being Quilp encourages Fred Trent's and Dick Swiveller's scheme to marry the latter to Nell as a part of his own generally wicked plans. He places Dick in a temporary job as a clerk to the lawyers, Sampson Brass and his sister, Sarah. They handle the mean and petty legal finaglings which are an essential element in Quilp's way of life.

The day before Quilp sells the Old Curiosity Shop out from under Nell and her grandfather, they run away from London to seek an idyllic life somewhere in the countryside. The elderly Mr. Trent is now so weak in wit and body that the child Nell is the responsible leader on the pilgrimage. The old man is forever fearful of being separated from Nell and locked up in a madhouse.

For a time the little girl and the old man find a relatively quiet refuge with Mrs. Jarley's waxworks. Mrs. Jarley takes a liking to Nell as everyone does who knows her. Mrs. Jarley employs her to show the wax figures of famous personages. This haven is destroyed when Grandfather Trent falls in with a couple of gamblers who revive his temporarily dormant mania for gambling. They encourage him to steal money from Mrs. Jarley in order to gamble more. The old man actually steals money from Nell herself. To frustrate the further temptation to steal Mrs. Jarley's money too, Little Nell leads her grandfather by the hand in another midnight flight from wickedness.

Their further flight is into a rising crescendo of hardship and deprivation in England's industrial midlands. Nell collapses from starvation, illness and exposure just as they meet an old and kind acquaintance, a schoolmaster whom they had met earlier in their journey. The schoolmaster is en route to a new job in a distant country village. He takes charge of Nell and her grandfather and they finally find the haven they have long sought. The schoolmaster is even able to provide a job for Nell as a guide to the occasional tourist who visits an old church and graveyard. For a time Nell's health seems partly restored, but the strain of their protracted flight has seriously undermined it, and she gradually begins to waste away.

The Trent's flight from the Old Curiosity Shop in London was so swift and secret that none of their former acquaintances has any idea what became of them. Indeed, Daniel Quilp feels sure they could not have done it without having some secret stock of money kept hidden from him. He makes a concerted effort to trace them to get from them what money they may still have. In addition to this enemy who is in pursuit of Nell and her grandfather, there is a friend who turns up in London about this time and coincidentally takes lodgings in the Brass' household. The "single gentleman" is actually Nell's great-uncle. He and his brother, Nell's grandfather, discovered that they loved the same girl, whom Nell's grandfather married and whom Nell greatly resembles. Thereupon the brother went off to

the colonies, where he solaced his broken heart by working hard, flourishing, and growing tolerably rich. Now he
has returned to seek reconciliation with his brother and
to help the family in any way he can with his money.

Little Nell and her grandfather are thus pursued in their
flight by the villain Quilp who wants to harm them, and by
a good angel, the single gentleman, who wants to succor
and save them. Although the two pursuers, the evil and the
good, occasionally cross each others' tracks in their pursuit
of the child and the old man they do not find Nell and her
grandfather.

Daniel Quilp meanwhile conspires with his legal ad-
visers, Sampson and Sally Brass, to frame Kit Nubbles,
who is working as a handyman with the Garland family.
Quilp hates everyone, but especially anyone good, and he
hates Kit in particular. His plot is successful and Kit is
wrongly accused and imprisoned. The plot was, however,
overheard by a small servant girl in the Brass household
who was befriended by Dick Swiveller and by him named
the "Marchioness."

After Kit's trial and conviction, Quilp decides he no
longer needs Dick Swiveller and orders Brass to fire him.
Dick, upset by Kit's misadventure, becomes dangerously
ill. He is nursed through this illness by the Marchioness,
who ran away from the Brasses to take care of Dick because he is the only person she has ever known who has
treated her with any sort of kindness. When he regains
consciousness the Marchioness tells Dick what she overheard in the Brass household. He sends her to the Gar-
lands and to their lawyer friend, Mr. Witherden, who together manage to exonerate Kit and trap the Brasses into
a confession. In an effort to serve his own interests by being
helpful to the cause of justice, Sampson Brass betrays

Quilp's role in the conspiracy. Quilp wanders out into the fog in an effort to escape arrest and falls into the Thames, and drowns.

Finally the single gentleman discovers the whereabouts of Nell and her grandfather and rushes off with Kit Nubbles to the remote village only to arrive just after Nell has died from the effects of her long suffering.

Barnaby Rudge

Barnaby Rudge is a mentally retarded boy whose best friend and playmate is a raven named Grip. It is generally believed that Barnaby's father was murdered shortly before Barnaby's birth. Actually Rudge murdered the man who was supposed to have murdered *him*. He changed clothes and other marks of identity and made sure that by the time the body was found it would be unidentifiably decomposed. Barnaby's mother, Mary Rudge, knows her husband lives, but no one else does. He wanders the earth a lonely incarnation of horror and guilt haunting his family and the novel.

The novel opens on the twenty-second anniversary of the murder. Old Rudge is actually present incognito in the "Maypole," a fabulous old country inn whose outstanding signpost is a thirty-foot high maypole. The inn is owned by a fat, dim-witted landlord named John Willet who is forever badgering his quite decent and normal son, Joe. The story of the murder is retold and then the mysterious stranger leaves for London late on a dark and stormy night. On his way he meets, and almost threatens, locksmith Gabriel Varden, who stops at the Maypole for some midnight cheer. Later Varden proceeds toward his home in London. On the way he encounters Barnaby who is

terribly upset at the blood on the wounds of young Edward
Chester who has been injured and robbed by old Rudge.
Rudge has proceeded to London where he occasionally
forces his wife to harbor him and give him money. Gabriel
Varden and Barnaby manage to bind up Chester's wounds
and take him to Mary Rudge's house to recuperate.

Gabriel then goes home to his wife, Martha. Originally
a very attractive woman, she has become something of a
harpy forever nagging her fun-loving husband with re-
pressive principles from the Protestant Manual. She is
aided and abetted in her hen-pecking by her servant Miggs.
Gabriel's adorable young daughter Dolly is the only attractive female person in the house, and even she is a terrible flirt and coquette with the young men.

Edward Chester is in a state of conflict with his father,
impoverished aristocrat John Chester, later *Sir* John, who
wants him to marry a rich heiress and support them both
in proper style. Young Ned is in love with Emma Haredale,
niece of Geoffrey Haredale, the Roman Catholic master
of the Warren, an estate near the Maypole. The Haredales,
though moderately well off, are not rich. Emma's father
Reuben was murdered on the same night as the man supposed to have been old Rudge. Most people believe the
double murder of Rudge and Reuben Haredale to have
been committed by the Warren gardner who then disap-
peared. There are those, however, who suspect that the
murders may have been done by Emma's uncle, Reuben's
brother Geoffrey, who inherited the Warren. Both murders were, of course, committed by Rudge.

Two other important characters are Varden's apprentice,
Simon Tappertit, a vain little fellow who thinks all
women, including his master's daughter Dolly, find the
beauty of his legs irresistible, and the Maypole ostler,
Hugh. Hugh is a mysterious, dark, strong, vicious, mean,

rugged, ugly customer whose origins are virtually unknown. His mother was a beautiful gypsy whom her son
saw hanged. Much later in the novel we learn he is actually
Sir John Chester's bastard son, but no one knows that at
this point. Like many other males in the novel, Hugh
has a hankering for Dolly Varden, and at one point he
comes very close to molesting her.

Geoffrey Haredale and John Chester have known and
cordially detested each other from early youth. Haredale
is Roman Catholic, Chester a Protestant. Haredale isn't
rich enough, in Chester's estimation, to make Emma a
suitable match for his son Edward. For these reasons
among others they agree that the young couple should be
kept apart.

Young love is nothing if not wilfully determined. Ned
and Emma find ways of communicating secretly with the
aid of Emma's good friend Dolly Varden, Ned's good
friend Joe Willet (who is glad to be cooperating with
Dolly Varden upon whom he dotes), and through the free-
roaming Barnaby Rudge.

Ultimately Haredale catches Edward and Emma together and forbids them to see each other. John Chester
employs Hugh as a spy to discover what his son and the
other young people are up to, and to aid in manipulating
them so they will become estranged from each other.
Finally John Chester forbids his son to consider Emma
further, when Edward insists on pursuing the lady he loves.
Thereupon John Chester disowns his son and forbids him
to come further into his presence.

Shameless flirt and coquette that she is, Dolly Varden
toys unmercifully with Joe Willet. When Joe's father makes
life for his son too intolerable, Joe runs away from the
Maypole to join the army and seek his fortune. He be-

comes a hero and loses an arm. Edward Chester in exile also distinguishes himself as a military officer.

Meanwhile Barnaby continues to enjoy Grip's companionship, pals around some with Hugh, whom he admires, and generally inhabits a world of dreams and fantasies. In the background, however, lurks the haunting fantastic presence of his father. Sim Tappertit joins and becomes captain of a secret society of apprentices who plan someday to foment revolution and take over the world. Their secret underground meeting place is presided over by a blind wretch named Stagg.

After a five year hiatus Lord George Gordon appears on the scene. Simple-mindedly monomaniacal, Gordon believes the ills of England are all caused by Roman Catholics. He is accompanied by stout-hearted John Grueby, and by a malevolent, manipulative private secretary named Gashford. He is the real brains behind the "No Popery" movement of which his master becomes the figurehead.

Ardent husband-baiting Protestant Martha Varden becomes a staunch financial supporter of the movement. Hangman Dennis joins the movement and so does Hugh. Sir John becomes a Member of Parliament to escape paying his debts. He manipulates Hugh and, to an extent, the "No Popery" movement from behind the scenes for his own personal ends. Sim Tappertit brings his revolutionary apprentices into the movement.

In an attempt to escape the persecutions of her husband, Mary Rudge has run away from London with Barnaby to seek a safe, anonymous harbor somewhere in the country. Their life is peaceful until Rudge, who has fallen in with the blind man, Stagg, finds Mary and her son. Rudge and Stagg force Mary and Barnaby to return to London. Foolish simple-minded Barnaby gets caught up in the Gordon Riots which are about to begin their anti-Catholic blood bath.

There are agitations and incidents in Parliament and outside it. Crowds begin to gather. The rioters destroy a number of Roman Catholic churches and shrines and begin persecuting Roman Catholic priests and lay people. At Sir John Chester's undercover instigation via Hugh, the rioters storm out of town to Haredale's Warren, and burn it to the ground. They rip up much of the Maypole Inn on the way, and of course cut down the maypole itself.

The rioters' next target is Newgate Prison. They want to free the prisoners there, among whom is old Rudge. He has finally been caught by persevering Haredale. At first the rioters capture locksmith Gabriel Varden and try to make him open the lock to Newgate's gate, a lock he helped design and build. Varden, who is on the side of the King and the militia against the lawless rioters, refuses. He barely escapes with his life. Two somewhat mysterious men come to his aid. One of them has only one arm. They appear to be rioters along with the rest, but they prevent Hugh from killing Varden.

The frustrated rioters then set fire to the gates to burn them down, but instead the fire spreads to Newgate prison. Near the conflagration at the prison is the house of an old purple faced vintner who did business with John Willet and the Maypole. Here the vintner and Haredale watch from the roof, until it becomes evident that the crowd will burn and destroy the vintner's house and warehouse, partly because he is opposed to their cause, and partly to get at the liquor. The spilled liquor ultimately forms a flaming lake in which dozens of frenzied alcoholic rioters drown and burn.

Meanwhile the old vintner and Haredale escape through the cellars and out the back way. On the way they meet the two mysterious strangers who turn out to be none other than Edward Chester and Joe Willet acting as undercover agents among the rioters. They bring with them Gabriel Varden whom they have saved from the rioters. Young Chester and Mr. Haredale are reconciled to each other.

Meanwhile Dolly Varden and Emma Haredale have been kidnapped by Hugh and Dennis and Sim Tappertit. Barnaby, temporarily captured and put in prison, meets his father, and joins him in his wanderings with Stagg after they all escape from prison.

Finally Haredale and Edward Chester and Joe Willet and Varden rescue the girls. Stagg and Rudge are killed. Barnaby, Hugh, and Dennis, among other villains, are caught and sentenced to hang. Varden and Haredale petition for Barnaby's pardon on the grounds of his simplemindedness, and he is saved from hanging at the last minute.

Geoffrey Haredale and Sir John Chester meet in a secluded country spot, argue, and fight a duel in which Haredale slays Chester. Haredale then exiles himself to the continent where he retires to a monastery.

Ned Chester marries Emma, Joe Willet marries Dolly Varden, and becomes landlord of the Maypole. The maypole itself is re-erected. Gabriel Varden is rewarded with the loving submission of his wife, Martha, who sees the error of her nagging Protestant Manual ways.

Martin Chuzzlewit

Martin Chuzzlewit is a novel about a terribly self-centered young man. Its central theme is "Interest" versus "Disinterest." As the novel opens Old Martin Chuzzlewit, the grandfather of the central figure of the same name, is sick and in great pain. He arrives with his young companion Mary Graham at the Blue Dragon, an inn operated by a young widow named Lupin. The Chuzzlewit clan, each more selfish and grasping than the next, arrives like vultures for a ghoulish conclave at the home of their relative, Mr. Pecksniff. At the meeting which ensues, phenomenally hypocritical Pecksniff triumphs and carries off the young heir apparent, Martin Chuzzlewit, to study architecture with him.

After a time in the Pecksniff household, young Martin and old Martin have a falling out about the younger Martin's insistent love for Mary Graham. The senior Martin banishes the young one and instructs Pecksniff to cast him out. Young Martin goes to seek his fortune in America. He takes masochistic Mark Tapley with him as his servant. Mark has left the felicities of service in the Blue Dragon whose landlady, Mrs. Lupin, clearly has a soft place in her heart for him. Mark is seeking moral and physical hardships to rise above with triumphant cheerfulness.

Young Martin Chuzzlewit is the second student Pecksniff cast out of his house. The first was John Westlock, of whom we shall hear more hereafter.

Enroute to America in steerage accommodations of the steamship, *The Screw,* young Martin thinks only of his own troubles. Mark thinks of nothing but the troubles of others, and is helpful to all. When they arrive in New York there are satiric encounters with American newspapers and American snobbery. They meet one decent sort of man, Mr. Bevan.

Martin and Mark go west seeking their fortune. There they are defrauded by General Cyrus Choke and by Zephaniah Scadder into investing their limited capital in land in "Eden." This ultimately turns out to be a fever-ridden totally undeveloped swampy place many days' journey away by river boat. They arrive in Eden, succumb to fever, and almost die. At a point near death a moral transformation occurs in Martin.

Back in England Pecksniff continues to pursue his hypocritical designs on old Martin's fortune. He takes old Martin, who appears to be incompetent and senile, into his home along with his nursemaid and companion, young Mary Graham. Mary is not related to the Chuzzlewits. That is why old Martin chose her for her intimate role. He has undertaken a rather Diogenes-like search for an honest, "disinterested" person. That has led him to establish with Mary an understanding that while he lives she will receive a competence, but that when he dies she has clearly no expectations whatsoever. Thus old Martin has sought to assure himself of disinterested care and attention. He trusts her. Pecksniff reads human nature differently. He expects that Mary, now that young Martin is out of the way, will inherit the bulk of old Martin's estate. Pecksniff therefore pursues young Mary Graham with all the ardor of a devoted suitor, but *much* against her inclination.

All of this old Martin watches with apparently incompetent eyes. At length Pecksniff's insistent, almost blackmailing attentions to Mary come to the notice of Tom Pinch, the most gullible of individuals. Tom, who loves to play the church organ and does it, during services, for nothing, has been the butt of everyone. More than anyone else, Tom has been taken in by Pecksniff, whose hypocrisy has up until now altogether fooled him. He now sees through Pecknsiff and is horrified. Pecksniff, quick to draw the first blood, expels him from his household, as he has already expelled John Westlock and Martin Chuzzlewit the younger.

On the same trip to London when Pecksniff convinced old Martin to put himself under his protection, Pecksniff also visited another rich and grasping Chuzzlewit, Anthony. Anthony Chuzzlewit has reared his only son, Jonas, on strict principles of self-interest. Soon thereafter Anthony dies, and Pecksniff, in his solicitude for the heir, Jonas, hires nurse Sarah Gamp to lay out the corpse for under-taker Mould.

Pecksniff had brought his two daughters, Charity, the elder, also know as Cherry, and Mercy, the younger, also known as Merry, with him to London and introduced them to their counsin, Jonas. Later Pecksniff brings Jonas home with him to recuperate from his grief. Jonas arranges for Sarah Gamp to care for his father's feeble-minded retainer and old friend, Chuffey.

Jonas seems to be paying court to the older girl, Cherry, but he is actually attracted to the younger, Merry, who is a tease. He enters into a sadomasochistic relationship with her which affords her a good deal of fun during their court-ship (she loves to make Jonas writhe), but which becomes a source of unrelieved misery for her when they are mar-ried.

One of the lesser hangers-on at the gathering of the Chuzzlewit clan at the beginning of the novel was im-poverished, threadbare, fraudulent Montague Tigg. When he becomes a successful confidence man in the "Anglo-Bengalee" insurance business he changes his name to Tigg Montague. On the strength of their relationship, Tigg manipulates Jonas Chuzzlewit's cupidity in such a way as to involve him financially in the Anglo-Bengalee company as a partner. He even prevails upon Jonas to get Pecksniff to invest most of his money in the company too.

Meanwhile Tigg's private detective Nadgett discovers that Jonas accelerated his father's terminal illness with poison. He learned this from Chuffey as well as from the pharmacist who supplied Jonas with the poison. The pharmacist is a distant acquaintance of John Westlock and he is nursed through a serious illness by Sarah Gamp. Tigg blackmails Jonas with this information and in the end Jonas murders Tigg too.

Tom Pinch went to London after he was expelled from the Pecksniff household. He set up housekeeping with his adorable little sister Ruth who had been dismissed from her miserable position as a governess in a *nouveau riche* industrialist's family. In London Tom sees his old friend, John Westlock, who has inherited a fortune. Westlock proceeds to fall in love with Ruth.

When young Martin and Mark Tapley return to England they go to Pecksniff's to see old Martin. Acting as old Martin's mouthpiece, Pecksniff rejects them. Mark is, however, received with open arms by his former mistress, young widow Lupin, and ultimately they marry.

Old Martin has in fact been *pretending* to be a mental incompetent. Secretly he has been giving Pecksniff enough rope to hang himself. He has been going through a spiritual inner change not unlike that of young Martin when he is near death in Eden. Both Martin Chuzzlewits become much less selfish and mercenary. Old Martin anonymously helps young Martin and Tom Pinch.

Ultimately John Westlock exposes Jonas as a criminal and Jonas commits suicide. Old Martin rejects Pecksniff, literally striking him down, and is reconciled to young Martin who marries Mary Graham with his blessing. John Westlock marries Ruth Pinch, and Tom happily returns to playing his organ.

David Copperfield

David Copperfield was born six months after the death of his father, who was also named David Copperfield. David's earliest childhood memories are of a sort of Garden of Eden existence in which he receives all of the attention and love of his beautiful young mother, Clara Copperfield, and of his less beautiful but equally loving housekeeper Clara Peggotty.

Into this idyllic existence comes the shadow of a suitor for his mother's hand. When dour and domineering Mr. Murdstone's suit prospers to the point of an imminent wedding, young David, without being told what is about to happen, is taken off to Yarmouth by Clara Peggotty. There they visit her brother, Daniel, whose nephew, Ham, and niece, Little Em'ly, are about David's age. David is welcomed into the bosom of this searfaring family which also includes Mrs. Gummidge, the widow of Peggotty's former partner. Little Em'ly becomes David's first love, after his mother.

When the happy Yarmouth interlude is over, David returns home to learn abruptly that he has a father—a stepfather, Mr. Murdstone. He identifies him with his father's gravestone in the nearby churchyard with which, in turn, he has vague, childish asociations of the story of Lazarus raised from the dead.

David at once cordially hates his stepfather who, with his equally cruel and grasping sister, Jane Murdstone, manages to make life quite miserable not only for David, but for his mother and for Clara Peggotty as well. In a childish fit of rage David bites Murdstone's hand, and is banished to a degraded school near London, Salem House, managed by a bully named Creakle. Here David meets two important friends, lovable Tommy Traddles and lordly, handsome James Steerforth.

Under Murdstone's oppressive treatment David's mother dies soon after the birth of a baby boy. The baby dies, too, and is buried with her in the same coffin and in the same graveyard as David's father. David learns of his mother's death on his birthday, and returns home for the funeral, leaving Salem House forever.

Murdstone dismisses Clara Peggotty, who goes off to marry a wagon driver named Barkis. After a short period of miserable loneliness and neglect living with the Murdstones, David is sent to London to begin work, at the age of ten. He earns a marginal living in a wine merchant's establishment, Murdstone and Grinby, in which Murdstone has an interest. David is here even more miserable and feels utterly abandoned. For a time he lives in a room in the family of an impecunious, pompous, lovable ne'er-do-well named Wilkins Micawber, who, after a period of time in a debtor's prison moves his family away to Plymouth.

David decides to run away too, but he doesn't feel able to impose himself upon Peggotty, now Mrs. Barkis, despite her abiding love for him. Returning to Murdstone is, of course, unthinkable. He decides to seek out his father's aunt, Miss Betsey Trotwood, who lives in Dover. She was present at his birth, but left in a huff when he turned out to be a boy. All of David's few possessions are stolen just before he leaves London, so he arrives on Miss Trotwood's doorstep in an utterly destitute condition.

Uncertain what to do with her uninvited grand-nephew, Betsey Trotwood takes him in for a few days, and writes to the Murdstones to come and consult with her. She develops an instant hatred for them upon their arrival to claim David. Miss Betsey finally decides to rear David as she had planned to do originally had he turned out to be a girl. She arranges through her lawyer and man of affairs, Mr. Wickfield, to send David to a very good school in Canterbury whose headmaster, Dr. Strong, is an excellent man and scholar. While he attends this school, David lodges with Mr. Wickfield, a widower, and his young daughter, Agnes. She looks after her father, and soon becomes like a sister to David. Wickfield's hypocritically humble, cringing, clammy clerk, Uriah Heep, fills David with revulsion.

David finishes school at the age of seventeen, and at Aunt Betsey's suggestion takes a modest traveling tour to see something of the world before settling upon a profession. He encounters James Steerforth again and is taken under Steerforth's somewhat condescending wing. Steerforth introduces David to his mother, a widow, and her companion, Rosa Dartle, a girl rendered striking by her intensely passionate, unrequited love for Steerforth. She is also marked by the ugly scar across her face Steerforth had put there with a bad tempered hammer when they were children.

In turn David takes Steerforth to Yarmouth to visit Clara Peggotty Barkis and her relatives there. Although beautiful little Em'ly is now engaged to her cousin, Ham, she and Steerforth are evidently attracted to each other. Steerforth begins to develop quite an interest in boating, fishing, yachting, and the waterfront generally.

David decides to enter law, and is articled to the firm of Spenlow and Jorkins. He promptly falls deeply in love with pretty, babyish Dora Spenlow.

Mr. Wickfield, meanwhile, has been gradually declining into a self-pitying alcoholic senility, encouraged by Uriah

Heep. By this time, Heep, who has become his partner, seeks to marry Agnes, but she will have none of him.

A number of tragedies now occur in rapid succession. David's secret engagement to Dora Spenlow is utterly spurned and rejected by her father, a widower who has acquired the services of Jane Murdstone as his daughter's companion. All of Aunt Betsey Trotwood's money, which had been managed by Mr. Wickfield, is apparently lost through bad investment. Wickfield becomes utterly dominated by his partner, Uriah Heep. Steerforth runs off with Little Em'ly, without marrying her. Dora's father drops dead abruptly, and, it turns out, leaves her penniless.

His hopes of a career in law utterly dashed, David becomes secretary to his former headmaster. Dr. Strong. Later he learns shorthand and becomes a newspaper reporter of parliamentary debates. During this period he has been in touch again with his old friend Tommy Traddles, who *has* successfully read for a career in law, and with his old friend Wilkins Micawber. For a time, Micawber becomes Traddles' landlord as he had been David's. Micawber later becomes law clerk to Uriah Heep.

Through this position Micawber manages to unravel Uriah Heep's criminal machinations in cheating Wickfield and his clients, like Aunt Betsey. Micawber exposes Heep's villainy and a partial financial restitution for Miss Trotwood and Mr. Wickfield ensues.

David's success as a reporter enables him to marry Dora, whose qualities as an erotic object are superb, but whose qualities as a housekeeper are miserable. Dora is not, in fact, mature enough for the responsibility of married life, and after a protracted period of illness and decline, she dies. Just before this tragedy occurs Wilkins Micawber emigrates to Australia. With him go Daniel Peggotty and

Little Em'ly whom Peggotty had finally been able to track down and locate after Steerforth abandoned her.

The world seems black indeed to David as he sets out on a European tour to try to overcome his deep sense of loss. Just before he leaves to go abroad he visits Yarmouth one more time to deliver Little Em'ly's last note to Ham. While there he witnesses an extraordinary storm which wrecks a ship within sight of the beach. Ham goes out heroically to try to save the one survivor who seems left on the ship clinging to a broken mast. He fails and drowns as does the man he tried to save, who turns out to be Steerforth.

After three years of licking his spiritual and psychological wounds on the continent, David returns home to Aunt Betsey. She cleverly manipulates David into discovering that he deeply needs Agnes Wickfield and that she had, of course, secretly loved him all through the long years. They marry. He becomes a successful novelist. They live happily ever after.

A Tale of Two Cities

As *A Tale of Two Cities* opens Mr. Jarvis Lorry of the banking house of Tellson and Company, which does business in both Paris and London, is enroute to France on a highly delicate mission. Dr. Alexandre Manette, who has been unjustly imprisoned in the Bastille for eighteen years, is to be restored to freedom and life in England. Mr. Lorry is aided in this endeavor by Tellson's villainous errand-runner and odd-job man, Jerry Cruncher, who sometimes literally moonlights as a "resurrection man." He steals fresh corpses from their graves for the use of physicians, medical students, and other anatomical researchers. Before board-

ing the ship to cross the channel, Mr. Lorry is joined by
young Lucie Manette, whose father has not seen her since
she was an infant.

In the St. Antoine district of Paris Dr. Manette waits,
rendered temporarily feebleminded by his long imprisonment. He thinks he is a shoemaker, and he is waiting in a
secret loft above the wine shop of M. Defarge. A large
wine cask has been dropped and shattered, and the starv-
ing residents of the district scrabble desperately to lick it
up from the street. The red wine looks like the blood which
will flow during the incipient revolution and its subsequent even more bloody Terror. Basilisk-like Mme. Defarge sits watching, knitting into a scarf the encoded
lengthy tale of aristocratic outrages which only the blood-
letting of the Revolution and the Reign of Terror will
ultimately unravel.

Five years pass. Dr. Manette has been restored to his
daughter. His mind has largely mended and he leads a
reasonably pleasant life in a secluded home in London. He
and Lucie have been called to the courtroom of the Old
Bailey to testify in the trial for treason of Charles Darnay.
Darnay is a teacher of French, and he seems both in language and in manner a perfect citizen of both the cities,
Paris and London. The case turns upon a matter of identification, and Darnay's attorney, Mr. Stryver, wins his
client's acquittal on the extraordinary circumstances that
his client looks exactly like his colleague, Sydney Carton.
Except for the fact that Carton's manner and grooming
are sloppy and careless, and Darnay's neat, the two men
are exact mirror images of each other.

There are other differences under the skin, too. Whereas
Charles Darnay is as energetic, hard working, sober, and
well disciplined in his life as he is in his manner and clothing, Sydney Carton is a drunken wastrel. He is a very

talented one, to be sure, for he is the legal brain behind Stryver's outstandingly successful courtroom career. He works up the cases and tells Stryver how to approach them, and what to say. For this brain work Stryver maintains him in all of his life-destroying bad habits, principally alcoholism.

The Manettes, father and daughter, after the trial admit Charles Darnay and Sydney Carton to their exceedingly quiet, not to say restricted, social circle, the one other inhabitant of which is Jarvis Lorry. The two young men buzz around Lucie like bees around honey, the one seriously and soberly pressing his suit, the other languidly and hopelessly.

Back in France the outrages of the aristocrats become increasingly insupportable. The Marquis de St. Evremonde, who is Darnay's uncle, is responsible for the death of a little peasant girl while driving his carriage furiously through a country town. Later he meets with his nephew in the family chateau. They quarrel bitterly. The Marquis is an implacable aristocrat while his nephew is burdened with a sense of guilt for the injustices committed by the family. Later that night the Marquis is murdered in his bed.

Back in England, Darnay, who has refused to accept his inheritance of the marquisate of St. Evremonde, asks Dr. Manette's permission to ask Lucie for her hand in marriage. He also seeks to tell Dr. Manette his true French name, but Manette asks him to wait until the wedding.

About this time Sydney Carton also asks Lucie to marry him. She graciously refuses him, and he tells her he would readily give his own life for her or hers if the need arose.

In France Gaspard is hanged for the murder of the Marquis. Mme. Defarge knits the St. Evremonde family into her endless scarf. The revolutionary society known as the "Jacquerie" burns the St. Evremonde chateau to the ground. News of Darnay's impending marriage to Lucie Manette reaches Defarge. He is unhappy to learn about this pending union between the child of a family hated by the revolutionaries and the child of a hero venerated by them.

Charles Darnay marries Lucie and tells his father-in-law that he is, in fact, the Marquis de St. Evremonde. The news, although apparently not altogether unexpected by Dr. Manette, is profoundly unsettling to him. He experiences a long mental relapse, and starts making shoes again. This has become his refuge at times of psychic stress or torment, especially if it is related to his interminable imprisonment.

Time passes. A little girl, young Lucie, is born to the Darnays. The Bastille is stormed, and Defarge finds some secret papers hidden by Dr. Manette in the cell in which he was imprisoned.

Tellson and Company, an international bank used by the French aristocrats in Paris, becomes something of a cross roads and message center for *émigrés* from Paris. While calling on Jarvis Lorry there, Charles Darnay learns of a letter addressed to the Marquis de St. Evremonde. He undertakes to deliver it to the proper person. No one knows it is he, except Dr. Manette, who is not about to tell anyone. The letter is from an old Evremonde family servant wrongly imprisoned by the revolutionary authorities. It begs the new Marquis to come to Paris to save him.

Out of honor, and against his good judgment, Darnay goes to Paris. He is almost immediately arrested as a hated aristocrat identified by Defarge. Jarvis Lorry is also in Paris at this time on Tellson business. Upon learning of Darnay's imprisonment, Dr. Manette and Lucie and little Lucie all come to Paris too. Dr. Manette is convinced that his credit with the revolutionary party will enable him to obtain his son-in-law's release. After more than a year, Darnay comes to trial. Partly because of his father-in-law's influence, and partly because he cannot be proven guilty, he is released. He is, however, forbidden to leave France. He is almost immediately rearrested. He is again accused by Defarge, and by one other person who is not named at that time.

Sydney Carton comes to Paris about this time to see if he can be of help to Lucie and her family. Also present in the city are Jerry Cruncher, the part-time ghoul, functioning as a general servant and aide-de-camp to Jarvis Lorry, and Miss Pross, Lucie's former nursemaid and utterly devoted servant. While shopping in Paris Miss Pross recognizes her long-lost brother Solomon, who turns out to be John Barsad. He is recognized by Cruncher as the former English spy who testified against Darnay at his trial in England. Carton and Cruncher hold over Barsad's head their knowledge that he is, or was, a double agent, spying for the English on one occasion, spying for the French on another.

Jerry Cruncher and Sydney Carton also recognize a man named Roger Cly who is with Barsad. Under an assumed name, Cly functions as a turnkey in the prison where Darnay is held. Cly was an even more despicable English spy than Barsad. To escape punishment in England he had pretended to die and be buried, so he could assume a false identity and get safely to France. Jerry Cruncher, on one of his nocturnal escapades to raise money by raising the dead, had excellent reason to know that Cly was not actually in the coffin buried under his name.

Darnay is tried, convicted, and sentenced to die on the guillotine for the crimes of his fathers (and uncle). The testimony is brought partly by Defarge whose wife's sister died after she was sexually abused by Darnay's uncle according to the aristocratic tradition of *le droit du seigneur.* Her peasant fiancé, who had tried to save her, was murdered by Evremonde. Dr. Manette, it now turns out, is a witness to these crimes because he was the medical man called in to attend them. He was thereupon confined to the Bastille on the strength of a dreaded *lettre de cachet* by the Evremonde influence. Dr. Manette is thus Darnay's other accuser because he wrote all this down on papers secreted in his cell. Doubly shocked by the revelation of these old secrets, which Dr. Manette had buried with the papers in his prison cell, and by his failure to save the husband of his beloved daughter, Dr. Manette relapses into shoemaking again.

Sydney Carton's moment to act has come. He goes to the Defarge wineshop and subtly establishes for all the revolutionaries the fact that there is in the Manette *menage* a young man who *looks very much like Darnay* and is a drunkard, but is really a totally different person, an Englishman. Taking advantage of his ascendency over Barsad and Cly, Carton gains admission to Darnay's cell the night before his execution. He drugs Darnay and takes his place. He has made arrangements with Jarvis Lorry for the immediate departure of the Manettes and their entourage as soon as the false, supposedly drunk "Carton" shows up delivered by Barsad to their waiting carriage. They all leave Paris, and France, safely, but not before Mme. Defarge, who would like to see the heads of all of them drop, has come to their apartment to make sure they are there. She finds only Miss Pross, doing some last minute packing and just about ready to leave. Miss Pross struggles with Mme. Defarge in order to prevent her giving any alarm. Mme. Defarge's revolver goes off, accidentally killing herself, and rendering Miss Pross deaf for the rest of her life.

Thus Mme. Defarge is after all cheated out of seeing

Evremonde, who is really Sydney Carton, guillotined. Carton thus redeems his promise to Lucie, and gains a permanent place in her heart he could have obtained in no other way.

Our Mutual Friend

The story of *Our Mutual Friend* opens with John Harmon on board ship returning to England from the colonies to inherit the millions his father made as a garbage, or dust, contractor in London. One of the ship's officers, George Radfoot, is aware that he himself bears a striking general resemblance to John Harmon. He knows that Harmon has been away from England for enough years so that no one at home would be likely to know *exactly* what he looks like. He plots to take Harmon's place, have Harmon murdered, and show up himself as the heir to the Harmon dust millions.

His plot is foiled, however, by another bunch of crooks who, unaware of Radfoot's plot, simply want to rob Harmon of the money he has brought back with him from the colonies. These thieves fall upon Radfoot and Harmon after they have exchanged clothes, murder the man they think is Harmon, and drop both bodies, the dead and the unconscious, in the Thames.

Harmon, dressed in Radfoot's clothes, manages to swim to shore, though drugged and slugged. The body of Radfoot, dressed as Harmon and carrying Harmon's identification papers, is fished out of the river a week or two later by a man who makes his living fishing bodies out of the Thames, Gaffer Hexam, and his daughter, Lizzie. The body is officially identified as being that of John Harmon, the heir to the Harmon garbage fortune.

On the evening that the Harmon body is found, a party is being given by *nouveau riche* Mr. and Mrs. Hamilton Veneering for their friends who, like everything else about them, are brand new. Among them are Melvin Twemlow, a great lord's poor relation; Lady Tippins, an antiquated society belle who obnoxiously tries to maintain the fiction of her youth and beauty; Mr. Boots and Mr. Brewer, who have made *their* new riches in those two respective trades; Mr. John Podsnap, a veritable colossus of the English upper middle class; Alfred Lammle, a gold-digger, and Sophronia Akershem, another of the same; and Eugene Wrayburn and Mortimer Lightwood, a pair of young lawyers of more or less independent means who are dilletantishly practising law and handling the Harmon Estate.

Mortimer amuses the dinner party by telling about the Harmon millions in dust and the extraordinary provisions of the Will. After specifying steps to ensure the corpse is truly dead before burial, the Will provides that young John Harmon, whom his father cordially hated, can inherit the money only if he marries a young lady (whom he does not know) named Bella Wilfer. If he fails to marry this particular young lady he inherits nothing and all the money goes to Mr. Nicodemus Boffin, formerly the elder Harmon's manager.

News of the discovery of the Harmon body arrives at the conclusion of Mortimer's recital and he and Eugene go to identify the body. They meet Gaffer Hexam. Eugene Wrayburn becomes promptly and thoroughly infatuated with Lizzie Hexam. Throughout much of the rest of the novel he devotes his considerable charm to attempting to seduce this beautiful, virtuous, dark haired girl.

At Gaffer Hexam's lodgings Mortimer and Eugene meet one Mr. Julius Handford, who pretends to be looking for someone *else* who may have drowned, but is really the real John Harmon *incognito*. Lizzie helps her exceedingly selfish brother, Charley, to run away against his father's will to go to school so he can rise in the world. One of his teachers later on, Bradley Headstone, a condensed incarnation of everything that is awkward and ugly, also becomes hopelessly infatuated with Lizzie, who won't have him either.

As their guest-list suggests, the Veneerings' world is an utterly false and superficial one of wealth. In the course of the novel Hamilton Veneering buys his way into Parliament. The Veneerings supervise the nuptials of Miss Akershem and Mr. Lammle. Afterwards Sophronia and Alfred Lammle each discover that the other is a gold-digger and that each has defrauded the other. They bitterly determine thereafter to work together to defraud the world around them.

They promote a plan for persuading Mr. Podsnap's daughter, Georgiana, to marry another money-grubbing acquaintance of theirs, "Fascination" Fledgeby. Fledgeby, a gentile, is the secret principal behind Pubsey and Company, a money lending firm. The front man for this company is a rather saintly Jew named Riah who is used by Fledgeby so he will be blamed for the sharp, mean, dishonest practices ordinarily associated in popular prejudice with Jews. Ultimately Riah escapes from Fledgeby and helps Lizzie Hexam. The Podsnap-Fledgeby match is spoiled. Fledgeby ruins the Lammles and is soundly beaten by Alfred.

As the novel opens Nicodemus Boffin and his wife, Henrietta, live in a house called "Harmony Jail." It is surrounded by immense mounds of dust which constitute the form of the Harmon capital at this point. Toward the end of the novel they are sold off and the garbage is transformed into money. Mr. Boffin, now the residuary legatee to the Harmon money, is illiterate, like Gaffer Hexam. He hires a wooden-legged man named Silas Wegg to read to him. Noddy Boffin, who comes to be known as the Golden Dustman, makes the first purchase with his new found wealth one of culture. Later, when Noddy and "Henerietty" move into a more suitable house for their wealthy station in life, they move Wegg into the former Harmon home to look after it, and, occasionally, to read to Noddy.

Silas Wegg meets Mr. Venus, a taxidermist and articulator of skeletons. He seeks him out in his search for bones of the leg which was removed in a hospital after an accident. Mr. Venus does a rather brisk business in body parts, human and animal, and gets Wegg his leg back. Wegg then hatches a plot with Venus to try to find around the Harmon house and its dust heaps another Will to supersede the one in force making Boffin residuary legatee. After many complications this plot is foiled toward the end of the novel because Mr. Venus decides to become friendly with Mr. Boffin and to help *him* rather than Wegg, who is a dreadfully nasty, mean man.

In addition to culture, the childless Boffins are interested in finding an orphan upon whom to expend their generosity. They want especially to find a little boy they can adopt and name John Harmon. They always loved the Harmon children throughout the period when they were being atrociously abused by their father. Their search is largely unrewarded. The one orphan they do find dies before they can arrange to adopt him. But they do acquire a Secretary and general man of business whose name is John Rokesmith, although he is really John Harmon *incognito*.

It has been John Harmon's intention from the very beginning to scout out Bella Wilfer without identifying himself, to see what kind of girl his wickedly unkind father has left him in his Will. To this end John Harmon has changed his assumed name from Julius Handford to John Rokesmith and rented a room in the Wilfer household. Harmon sees that Bella is bewitchingly beautiful, but impossibly spoiled and self-willed. He falls head over heels in love with her, while realizing that she would be a dreadful person to marry. Bella is much too mercenary to consider marrying anyone who isn't rich, especially after having had her expectations raised by the elder Harmon's Will.

John Harmon is aware that were he to reveal his identity and marry Bella she would marry him only for his money. The money would forever stand between them and prevent their loving each other as people. John and Bella's problem is analogous to Eugene and Lizzie's, and to Alfred and Sophronia's. The Lammles each married for money without really loving each other. They are caught in a bitter relationship which has neither love nor money. Eugene is in love with Lizzie but is afraid that if he marries someone so far below him socially, his father will disinherit him and he will thus have love without money. John is afraid that if he marries Bella they will have money, but without love. Therefore he seeks to find a way to win her love without revealing himself to be the heir to the Harmon money. He will marry her (and thereby get the money his father has willed him *with* her) only if she will love him for himself *without* the money. But she is initially much too spoiled and pampered and mercenary to consider anything of the sort. His father, who always hated his son, has found a diabolically ingenious way to torture his son even after he is dead.

Mr. and Mrs. Boffin, well aware that they have now inherited money which would have been Bella Wilfer's had John Harmon lived and married her, want Bella to benefit from the money even if John is dead. So they invite Bella to live with them in their splendid new home and to lead the kind of life the Harmon money can provide. It is while he is making these arrangements with the Wilfers that Mr. Boffin, who has just employed Rokesmith as his secretary, refers to him as "our mutual friend." In the course of time the mere secretary, Rokesmith, makes clear to the adopted heiress, Miss Wilfer, that he loves her. She rejects him with scorn as being utterly beneath her.

Soon after this Mrs. Boffin's loving intuition enables her to guess John Rokesmith's true identity. The Boffins, overjoyed to find John Harmon, the orphan for whom they have been searching, alive, help him to find a way to teach Bella to love him for himself. Noddy Boffin undertakes to pretend to succumb to a miserly love of money. He has Wegg endlessly read him the lives of the misers as though they were the lives of the saints. More and more he reveals how unattractive is the mere love of money. More and more he begins to praise those very mercenary qualities in Bella which are her only blemishes, and which render her incapable of considering the love of anyone, like Rokesmith, without money. Gradually Noddy's behavior teaches Bella to regard those mercenary qualities she had once viewed as being right and proper in herself as being ugly moral shortcomings. The crisis comes when Noddy pretends to expel Rokesmith from his house and from his employment for daring to look above himself toward Bella. He praises Bella for having the proper spirit and pride to reject Rokesmith's impertinent advances.

Finally Bella, for all that she has come to love Mr. and Mrs. Boffin very much, can no longer accept what appear to be their mercenary qualities. She rejects these qualities and at the same time rejects all the old aspects of herself which the Boffins' pretended miserliness made evident to her. Bella leaves the Boffin household, and realizes that in her heart she really does love John Rokesmith very much for himself. She goes after him, finds him with her father, and becomes engaged to him. John and Bella marry and live happily together for a long time, indeed, until after the birth of their first child, a daughter, before John finally reveals who he is. At that point they enter into their inheritance. And so John Harmon has effected a singular fulfillment of his father's Will.

Meanwhile, although Eugene Wrayburn cannot bring himself to risk his father's displeasure by proposing marriage to Lizzie Hexam, neither can he stop trying to seduce her. By this time Lizzie has lost her father, who, while fishing for corpses one night, fell overboard, got tangled in his own line, and hanged himself accidentally under water. His boat drifts back dragging his corpse behind it much as it has dragged so many other corpses.

For a time Lizzie lives with Jenny Wren, a young crippled girl who earns her living making dresses for dolls. Lizzie secretly loves Eugene, but she will not accede to his dishonorable attempts to make her his mistress. She does *not* love Bradley Headstone, her brother's former teacher and present colleague, and her brother disowns her for her unwillingness to marry the man who has helped his career.

With the help of Riah, Lizzie runs away from London and seeks to hide both from Headstone and from Wrayburn. But Eugene finally discovers where she is and follows her. He, in turn, is followed by Bradley, who, insanely jealous, attempts to murder him. The attempt is almost successful. Beaten about the head, Eugene falls in the river and is almost drowned. Lizzie, who is, after all, experienced at pulling drowned people from rivers, saves him. For a long time Eugene hovers between life and death. Lizzie and Jenny Wren nurse him gradually back to life. He is morally transformed, and decides, regardless of his father's will in the matter, to do the right thing and to marry Lizzie. It turns out that his father approves the union, so he, too, winds up with both love and money.

Only one person has proof of Headstone's murderous attempt. This is Roger Riderhood, better known as "Rogue" Riderhood. A thorough-going villain, Riderhood had at one time worked with Hexam in the corpse fishing business. He was actually implicated in the Radfoot-Harmon murder, but he accused Gaffer Hexam of being guilty of that crime. Before leaving the Thames waterfront Riderhood was nearly drowned by a steamer. He is only just barely brought back to life. In order to end his attempts at blackmail, while at the same time ending his own tortured and frustrated existence, Bradley Headstone drowns both himself and Riderhood by locking his arms around Riderhood and plunging into the canal lock.

BIBLIOGRAPHY

AMONG ALL OF the various writings of Sigmund Freud probably the most valuable background for this book is provided by his earliest, and in some ways most seminal work, *The Interpretation of Dreams.*

Charles Dickens published his novels in monthly installments, with the exception of *Hard Times,* which was published in weekly numbers. The publication of a novel thus occurred throughout a year, and sometimes two years, at the completion of which the whole novel was published in volume form. The chronology is as follows:

Pickwick 1836-1837
Oliver Twist 1837-1838
Nicholas Nickleby 1838-1839
Old Curiosity Shop 1840
Barnaby Rudge 1841
Martin Chuzzlewit 1843-1844
Dombey and Son 1846-1848
David Copperfield 1849-1850

Bleak House 1852-1853
Hard Times 1854
Little Dorrit 1855-1857
A Tale of Two Cities 1859
Great Expectations 1861
Our Mutual Friend 1864-1865
The Mystery of Edwin Drood 1870

Among the bewildering variety of biographies of Dickens two are preeminent. The most recent definitive work is Edgar Johnson, *Charles Dickens: His Tragedy and Triumph* (New York, Simon and Schuster, 1952). The other, which stands in its own right among the world's great works of biography, is that by Dickens' friend, John Forster, *The Life of Charles Dickens* (London, Cecil Palmer, n.d.)

Edmund Wilson's essay "Dickens: The Two Scrooges" in *The Wound and the Bow: Seven Studies in Literature* (New York, Oxford University Press, 1941) provides one of the earliest applications of psychoanalysis to this author. Steven Marcus *Dickens: From Pickwick to Dombey* (New York, Basic Books, Inc., c.1965) is essential background reading for this book. It provides one of the hitherto most extensive applications of psychoanalytic method to Dickens. Two other recent valuable critical works are J. Hillis Miller, *Charles Dickens: The World of His Novels* (Cambridge, Massachusetts, Harvard University Press, 1965) and Taylor Stoehr, *Dickens: The Dreamer's Stance* (Ithaca, New York, Cornell University Press, c.1965).

And no serious student of Dickens can afford to overlook *The Dickensian,* published monthly by the Dickens Fellowship 1905-1918, and quarterly 1919 to the present.

INDEX